I am delighted that communities across Britain are taking the opportunity of the Golden Jubilee to mark fifty years in the life of our nation. I see it as an occasion both to celebrate the past and to look forward with hope to the future; we are a resourceful people and I believe our long history and traditions help to give us the confidence to find new and creative ways to respond to the challenges ahead.

I am grateful to all of you who have given Prince Philip and me such loyal support over these fifty years. It has always been a great strength to know from all those I meet and the letters I receive that you have been with me, through good times and bad, as I have tried to the utmost of my ability to serve this country and the Commonwealth. It has been an honour to do so.

Elizabeth R

ST. JAMES'S PALACE

Golden Jubilees have happened rarely in our history. They celebrate something very special: not only the life, the service and the contribution of a Sovereign over half a century, but also the continuity of our traditions and institutions and the unique role they play in helping to define some of the deeper aspects of our common identity. I, for one, believe that the dedication and service of The Queen over the last fifty years have touched and enhanced the lives and spirits of countless people, both in the United Kingdom and in the Commonwealth and around the world. Her Majesty's life and work have symbolised and given a powerful expression to those very qualities of selflessness and duty which are the mark of a truly civilized society. These are important reasons in themselves, to say nothing of the opportunity to enjoy a series of very special events over the coming months, to be celebrating Her Majesty's Golden Jubilee.

Cover photograph by HRH The Duke of York

Piccadilly, 1952

No longer an island

Fifty years in the life of the nation
by Godfrey Smith

On 7 February 1952 *The Times,* which contained 12 pages and cost 3d, carried a two-line headline at the top of page one. It read: DEATH OF THE KING and measured one and a quarter inches wide by half an inch deep. The rest of the front page was filled as usual with small ads. There was a lively demand for cooks at £4 to £5 a week and parlour maids at £3.10s. It seemed, for readers of *The Times,* as if little had changed since 1939. It was a world filled with what the poet Louis MacNeice called the inter-ripple and resonance of years of dinner gongs. But appearances were deceptive.

When the Queen came to the throne, the weekly wage of a manual worker in manufacturing was £7.58. Yet during the 1950s it roughly doubled to £14.82. At the start of the decade petrol was still rationed and food still on points. At one moment in the 1950s the fresh meat allocation was worth 8d a week, and there was still a five-shilling limit in restaurants. All these legacies of war were swept away by the end of the decade. It was, as Harold Macmillan laconically put it, the time when we never had it so good.

The island race took enthusiastically to exotic new manias from abroad like espresso coffee and rock'n'roll. People rushed to read *Lucky Jim*, the keynote novel in which Kingsley Amis introduced us to a new kind of oafish anti-hero. Then in May 1956 the astonished audience at a new play called *Look Back in Anger* at the Royal Court Theatre, saw the curtain rise on an attic flat somewhere in the Midlands. Here Alison Porter ironed dutifully while her unappetising husband Jimmy railed against everything she stood for in a virtuoso exercise of unleashed venom. It spelled farewell for the bland fare served in Shaftesbury Avenue. John Osborne had smashed the mould.

Yet there were traditional heroes too. Roger Bannister became the first man to run the mile in under four minutes; and it was the era of the great British playboy racing drivers – Hawthorn, Collins and Moss. It was also the era of the great traitors: Pontecorvo, the atomic physicist, defected to Russia while the diplomats Burgess and Maclean, who had disappeared in 1951, resurfaced there four years later. We did not then know that two more traitors, Blunt and Philby, members of the same charmed circle, still lurked undetected within the British Establishment.

With hindsight, the opening years of the Queen's reign look modest and monochrome. Footballers earned only £12 a week and it cost £318 to send a boy to Eton. There were 344,000 TV licences in 1950 and it was the coronation which sent people scrambling to buy TV sets. But they saw it in black and white; colour TV did not begin till 1968. The launch of ITV in 1955 gave a welcome jolt to the BBC, though many companies who launched it were to suffer grievous losses before it became clear, in Roy Thomson's crisp words, that they had a licence to print money.

It was a murky world as well. Smog, which had caused thousands of deaths, was swept away by the Clean Air Act of 1956. People discovered that they lived not in cities of black marble, but sandstone and limestone. The first motorway, the M1, opened in 1959 and cut the journey from London to Birmingham in half. Altogether 2,100 miles of motorway were to be built in the 50 years to cope with the avalanche of cars on our roads: 1.75 million in 1952; 27 million now. But we ripped up 20,000 miles of railway track. The net result is that we have the most congested roads and strangled cities in the world.

Nothing could have been more radically different than the taste and feel of the 1960s. They began with the hope of a new Camelot as John F Kennedy took office. They were seasoned at home by the launch of a new satirical movement of anarchic power. *That Was The Week That Was* thumbed its nose at the Establishment on TV each week under the liberalising beneficence of the new BBC director-general, Hugh Carleton Green. Four formidably gifted young men brought their smash hit review *Beyond The Fringe* from Edinburgh to London and took the mickey out of concepts previously sacrosanct: patriotism, religion, monarchy. Then in 1963 four more young men who called themselves The Beatles were to enchant the world and be hailed by one serious critic as the greatest songwriters since Schubert.

The 1960s saw Mary Quant lead the craze for the mini-skirt and a new wave of working class photographers – Duffy, Donovan, Bailey – take centre stage. It was the heyday of Carnaby Street and King's Road. At the Old Bailey it was decided – in a trial of high drama and comedy – that *Lady Chatterley's Lover* was not obscene. The contraceptive pill went on sale for the first time. Abortion became legal and so did homosexual acts between consenting adults in private. The Profumo Affair was compulsively entertaining but damningly subversive too. It was the era of psychopathic criminals like the Krays and Richardsons; underworld icons who seemed to move effortlessly in and out of high society. The surrealist nature of the decade culminated in 1969 with the world-conquering *Monty Python* show.

In brutal contrast the assassination of John F Kennedy unfolded horrifyingly on the TV sets which now graced most homes. The building of the Berlin Wall in 1961 gave concrete reality to the gulf between capitalism and communism. There was a spate of spy sensations – Philby, Blake, Vassall – that seemed to mirror only too faithfully the fictional world of the great spy writers – Deighton, Le Carré and Fleming. The Western world was not at ease with itself; the alliance of workers and students in France in a month-long battle at the barricades sent ripples of unrest across the Channel and indeed the world. When the Conservative minister Enoch Powell made his notorious speech prophesying rivers of blood he was sacked by Edward Heath; but it had focused attention on the need for a viable immigration policy, which recognised our enrichment in becoming a multi-cultural society nourished by many faiths. Industrious Asian families, for example, have brought convenience to our lives by keeping their corner stores open all hours. And nearly a third of our doctors were not born here.

DECADES HAVE AN UNCANNY GIFT for defining themselves. That perceptive writer Christopher Booker, for example, has argued that the 1970s were "the decade when our bluff was called". It was the era of Watergate and the first resignation in office of an American president. There was the humiliating shambles of Vietnam, the agony of Cambodia, and the worst economic recession since the war. Here inflation rose at one point to 24 per cent and the Prime Minister, Harold Wilson, warned of "a catastrophe of unimaginable proportions". After the long, delirious rave-up of the 1960s came the monster hangover. A series of strikes by the low-paid was a stark reminder that modern societies need such workers. Hospitals were closed, ambulances failed to run, water shut off, sewage untreated and bodies unburied. A more bitter aftermath to the Swinging Sixties it would be hard to imagine.

The Conservatives were in power for 34 years of the half century, Labour and New Labour for a little less than half as long. In those years our politicians were marinated in a series of cataclysmic crises. The Suez adventure separated fathers and sons, husbands and wives as no other issue had done since the Boer War. The Cuban missile crisis brought the world within a whisker of nuclear war for 10 nightmare days. In Ireland Bloody Sunday saw the deaths of 13 unarmed Catholic protesters, shot by British soldiers, and cast its dark shadow forward to the present day. Then in 1982 the Falklands conflict saw a British task force set out once more for what would surely be the last of our colonial wars. It cost a million pounds to free each man, woman and child on the Falklands and, infinitely more precious, the lives of nearly a thousand young men.

It was, however, a crushing triumph for Margaret Thatcher, and may well have been instrumental in sweeping her back to power again in 1983. In all she was to lead the country for more than 11 years. She seemed perfectly cast for the 1980s as the world swung radically right. In America President Reagan was her natural ally. She fought bruising power battles with the miners and the print unions and won them both. While she was at No. 10, the smack of firm government resounded through the land. She presided triumphantly over the era of the Big Bang and the Golden Hello. The yuppie, or young urban professional, made his bow and found his

apotheosis in Nick Leeson, the derivatives dealer from nowhere who made a fortune for Baring's till his luck changed, sending them to perdition and himself to jail. He was at best, though, a bit player in the drama that shook the upper-middle class to its foundations. Stately homes were snapped up by those who had struck it rich in commodities and currencies, from those who had effortlessly lost the lot at Lloyd's.

The Queen was not immune from the storms that buffeted her subjects. She had to cope with the loss of Lord Louis Mountbatten, beloved uncle Dicky to her family, murdered by the IRA, and the tidal wave of national grief caused by the death of Princess Diana. She was to see the marriages of her sister and three of her children founder. On the other hand her own marriage has proved admirable in its stability. And the Queen Mother, one of 12 centenarians to receive the usual royal telegram of congratulation on her 100th birthday in August 2000, proved to be a bedrock of unquantifiable value. Nor can there be any doubt about the exemplary way the Queen has presided over our long evolution from Empire to Commonwealth and from Britons to Europeans. After decimalisation in 1971, we had taken our first tentative step to becoming Europeans when we joined the Common Market in 1973 under the Heath government, but when the Queen opened the Channel Tunnel with President Mitterand on 6 May 1994, two centuries after it was first mooted, the symbolism was clear. We were no longer an island.

IT WOULD BE AGREEABLE to discern in the 1990s echoes of the gaiety that so famously marked the 1890s. But each decade spawns its own disasters; this time, the Gulf War and the onset of ethnic cleansing in Bosnia. In Britain, however, those looking inward at our domestic quality of life saw the customary chequered pattern. The coming of the credit card and the liberalisation of lending destroyed thrift but underwrote the consumer society. Home computers, unthinkable at the start of the reign, are now in two houses in five; video recorders in nine out of ten. But our inner cities are a battlefield and our countryside, denuded of ditches and hedges by the demands of large-scale farming, has lost its distinctive, quilted charm. Our country pubs remain a delight but six a week are closing.

After the first 50 years of the Queen's reign her subjects are far wealthier. We send three times as many to prison but no longer hang people. Class is dwindling to a joke; style has taken over. We live eight years longer; divorce five times more. Yet we remain the tolerant and civilised place that has given the world great humanitarian agencies such as Amnesty International and Oxfam. We are still a haven for refugees from less happy lands and a hospitable showplace for new talent from every corner. We can still laugh at ourselves. So there is much to celebrate.

Godfrey Smith, journalist and author, is a columnist on The Sunday Times

Piccadilly, 2002

First, a Princess

A year before her engagement *to Prince Philip of Greece, Princess Elizabeth, aged 20, posed for this portrait (right) in Buckingham Palace in 1946.*

Princess Elizabeth was the child of a very close-knit family, always proudly referred to by her father, the then Duke of York, as "Us four". In this family portrait (above), the Duchess has the five-month old Princess Margaret on her knee and Princess Elizabeth was aged five. The Duke became King George VI in 1936 when his brother, Edward VIII abdicated to marry an American divorcee, Mrs Wallis Simpson. Princess Elizabeth became heiress to the throne when she was 10, a year after this portrait of her in a reflective mood was taken (right).

The princesses dressed identically until they were in their late teens. Princess Elizabeth is 16 in this photograph (below) and Princess Margaret is 11. King George VI, as a younger brother who had suffered age discrimination, was determined that the four years separating his daughters should as far as possible be ignored.

No. 230873 Second-Subaltern Elizabeth Alexandra Mary Windsor (below) completed a driving and vehicle maintenance course with the Auxiliary Territorial Service (ATS) in 1945 and qualified as an Army driver. Biographer Sarah Bradford wrote that the 19-year-old Princess "longed to go out and acquire a skill... to 'do her bit' for the war effort". She loved her brief service in the ATS and many years later said that it was the first time that she was able to test her capabilities against women of her own age.

The handsome naval officer with a distinguished war record became Princess Elizabeth's fiancé in July 1947 (left), when she was 21 and he was 26. The princess had first met Prince Philip of Greece, a prize-winning cadet at the Royal Naval College, Dartmouth, on a royal visit there when she was 13. He was mentioned in despatches during the war, and at 21, as a first lieutenant, he was second in command of a destroyer covering the Allied landings on Sicily in 1943 – the youngest officer in the Royal Navy holding such a post.

The Princess was married to Prince Philip at Westminster Abbey (right) on 21 November 1947, the day on which he was created Prince Philip, Duke of Edinburgh. However, the King's wish to keep this title of a British prince a surprise meant that Philip's name on the order of service was simply 'Lieutenant Philip Mountbatten, RN'.

Their honeymoon days were divided between Broadlands, 'Uncle Dickie' Mountbatten's home in Hampshire (below) and Birkhall, the Princess's pre-war family holiday home at Balmoral, Scotland.

The reign begins in an age of austerity

When Princess Elizabeth became Queen in 1952 the country was still in the grip of austerity in the wake of the Second World War. Food, clothes and fuel continued to be rationed. But the coronation, in 1953, made London "a city of light and happiness and radiant hope" said the Daily Mail

Commentary by Peter Crookston

The façade of the Tivoli (above) near Piccadilly Circus and the misspelling in the film poster are signs of the tired condition of the country in the early Fifties. But good news cheered up people on the eve of the coronation: a British expedition, led by Col. John Hunt, reached the top of Mount Everest. Edmund Hillary, from New Zealand, and Tenzing Norgay, a Sherpa from Nepal, were the first to stand on the summit. Television went nationwide for the first time in coronation year: more than 20 million people in Britain watched the BBC's live broadcast from Westminster Abbey on 2 June 1953 – an average of 10 people per set.

The Queen's Christmas message to the Commonwealth, already familiar on radio, was televised for the first time in 1957, from Sandringham (left).

The Queen's official portrait (right) was also taken in 1957 by the photographer Antony Armstrong-Jones. He was later to marry Princess Margaret and be given the title Earl of Snowdon.

Two photographs of the Queen taken in 1959 show typical moments in her working day: **Inspecting** *a guard of honour (left) of the Irish Guards at Stormont, Northern Ireland, while on a tour of the province;* **At her desk** *(below) in Buckingham Palace after dealing with one of the daily boxes of Government documents.*

Wearing her robes and the heavy Imperial State Crown –
which was on her head for three hours after the coronation – the Queen was photographed (left) by Cecil Beaton with her maids of honour in Buckingham Palace when she returned from Westminster Abbey. They were Lady Moyra Hamilton, Lady Mary Baillie-Hamilton, Lady Jane Heathcote-Drummond-Willoughby, Lady Anne Coke, Lady Jane Vane-Tempest-Stewart and Lady Rosemary Spencer-Churchill. Later that year, the Queen and the Duke of Edinburgh set off on a tour of the Commonwealth, travelling 43,618 miles and making the first visit by a reigning monarch to Australia and New Zealand. They returned in May 1954. Two months later rationing stopped in Britain – nine years after the end of the war.

Stanley Matthews *shook hands with the Queen (right) after Blackpool's 4-3 victory over Bolton at Wembley in 1953 – the first football match she attended. It was the third time he had played in a Cup Final, but the first in which he received a winner's medal. Matthews, a modest role model to a whole generation of boys who tried to emulate his mesmerising dribbling skills, was to meet the Queen again in 1965 when she knighted him for services to football.*

Marilyn Monroe, *who was in London making 'The Prince and the Showgirl', was introduced to the Queen (left) at a Royal Command Performance of 'The Battle of the River Plate' in October 1956. In that same month a real battle was fought by British and French forces invading Port Said, following the nationalisation of the Suez Canal by Egypt's President, Col. Nasser. Pressure from the United States and the UN, the collapse of sterling and deep unease in Britain about the invasion, forced an Anglo-French withdrawal from Suez a month later. Prime Minister Anthony Eden, his health broken by the crisis, resigned in January 1957.*

At Balmoral *(right), before leaving for her six-month tour of the Commonwealth, the Queen and the Duke of Edinburgh had a long holiday with their children in the summer of 1953, where Princess Anne, helped by the Queen and Prince Charles, pioneered a new way to enter the castle. The Prince and Princess were left in the care of the Queen Mother during the tour.*

It is indeed a great joy, as well as an honour, to be able to write this in

celebration of Her Majesty's Jubilee Souvenir Programme. We have always treasured Her Majesty's support and we are deeply appreciative of all that Her Majesty has done to help South Africans on their journey in building a better life for themselves. Her Majesty Queen Elizabeth II has played a very particular historical role in helping South Africa in its re-entry on to the world stage. Her Majesty spared no efforts in helping to open doors that were once shut to South Africa and to South Africans.

Her Majesty's support of me as the first democratically elected President of South Africa greatly impacted on me personally and on South Africa as a nation. Her Majesty's active support in my first few years as President helped to increase British trade and investment into South Africa, helping the South African government to begin to address the economic and social imbalances that we inherited.

Her Majesty has helped ensure that the Commonwealth does not become stagnant in its thinking and has guided it to move with change and not against it. It is this leadership that has helped to make the Commonwealth as relevant and as needed as it was when it was formed in 1949.

As head of the Commonwealth, Her Majesty played a very important role in South Africa's readmission into the organisation. The re-admittance of South Africa into the Commonwealth has helped give our country a sense of being part of an international community. Our re-admittance also helped to refocus attention on the plight of the poor in the developing world. And give a new urgency to redressing the social, economic and political inequalities that exist in many of the Commonwealth members.

South Africa has always treasured her membership of an organisation which spans continents and brings together a group of diverse nations whose purpose is to promote international understanding, world peace and prosperity.

As we move forward in the 21st century, the Commonwealth of Nations has a very important role to play in helping millions of people across the globe to fight the scourge of HIV/AIDS and live free of poverty and war.

We would like to thank the Commonwealth members; under the wise leadership of Her Majesty, they have been able to face many daunting challenges.

18 March 2002

Nelson Mandela

Nelson Mandela

The Oba of Lagos Adeniji Adele II welcomes the Queen to Nigeria (left) in 1956, at the beginning of her three-week tour of the country with the Duke of Edinburgh, during which they visited a leper colony.

On tour a fanfare was blown for the Queen (below) at a ball in Fiji, the Commonwealth nation in the South Pacific, receiving the first visit in its history by a British sovereign. The royal tour began in November 1953, as British troops were beginning to return from Korea. The war there – in which they served with the United Nations force and supported American troops – ended in July 1953. But British troops were then deployed in Kenya to cope with the Mau Mau insurrection.

At King's College Hospital, *London, a young patient was lifted up to the Queen's car window (above) to present a bouquet after she opened a new wing there in 1953. Hospitals were a rebuilding priority as the National Health Service expanded, five years after its founding by the post-war Labour Government.*

New council housing *proliferated as the rebuilding of Britain went on apace in the early Fifties. The Queen opened a new estate at Crawley, Sussex, in 1953 and while visiting a tenant, lorry driver Eric Hammond, his neighbours had a close-up view over the garden wall (right). The Conservative Government's Minister of Housing, Harold Macmillan (later to be Prime Minister 1957-63), pushed through the largest local authority house-building programme ever seen in Britain, with more than 300,000 new homes built every year between 1951 and 1954.*

Winston Churchill, *who led Britain throughout the worst days of the war, and became Prime Minister again in 1951, gave a dinner for the Queen on his retirement in 1955, after which he escorted her to her car as she left 10 Downing Street (above). They had known each other throughout the war, when Churchill was a frequent visitor to Buckingham Palace. Their close aquaintance was renewed at his weekly prime ministerial audiences. Sir Winston, also an enthusiastic racehorse owner, said that when Government business was over they talked mostly about racing. As the Fifties ended and a new decade began, the Queen met two other great wartime leaders – she shared the opening ceremony of the St Lawrence Seaway in 1959 with US* **President Eisenhower,** *(top right) who had been Supreme Allied Commander in Europe. And in 1960* **General de Gaulle**, *who led the Free French government in London during the war, made a State Visit (right) as President of France.*

In the kind of Daimler *that swished up gravel drives of the Home Counties in John Betjeman's poetic idylls,*
the Queen arrives at the Royal Windsor Horse Show in 1957 with the eight-year-old Prince Charles and six-year-old
Princess Anne. It was the year in which Prince Charles's formal education began, at Hill House prep school in
Knightsbridge. He was the first heir to the throne to attend school. The Prince later became a boarder at his father's
old school, Gordonstoun, in Scotland, and Princess Anne became a pupil at Benenden in 1963.

Design for living

by Terence Conran

THE LAST 50 YEARS have been a period of cataclysmic change in style and taste, more so than any other period in our history. One of the major events that kick-started this change was the Festival of Britain in 1951, which heralded the beginning of the modern movement. The Festival, with its exciting plans for rebuilding Britain gave people optimism about the way we could live our lives. By the time Princess Elizabeth was crowned in 1953, rationing had almost ceased and people found they had a bit of money in their pockets. There was more information available about the world around us – television became affordable, foreign travel, previously the domain of the rich, was becoming more accessible. Magazines showed that there was an alternative lifestyle to that of one's parents. People, particularly the urban young, were looking for change.

The way the newly affluent twenty- and thirty-somethings inhabited their homes had altered by the late Fifties. What they wanted were new modern furnishings. The kitchen was becoming more of a focal point. Fitted units were replacing dressers. Modern materials were appearing – linoleum and leather were being substituted with vinyl, oilcloths and linen with Formica and other laminates. Open-plan living was gaining ground, central heating meant that the fireplace was no longer necessary. Three-piece suites, hi-fi consoles and televisions were given priority in these homes. Bathrooms, too, changed radically. The outside loo gave way to heated towel-rails and matching sanitary ware in a full spectrum of pastels. In furniture the influences of the Bauhaus and William Morris were at last available on a modest scale and at a competitive price. At Habitat shoppers could choose everything needed for the modern home, from furniture and fabrics to cookware and cutlery. On the Continent, Ikea took this ideal of democracy and spread the word worldwide.

From the austerity of the post-war early Fifties, the gamut has run from French Provençal, with Souleiado providing the yellow and azure prints, to Laura Ashley florals, to Biedermeier classicism, to Jim Thompson supplying the demand for Thai silks. The English country house look of Colefax and Fowler and their acolytes was seen in the suburbs, from Wimbledon to Wilmslow. Italian sleek, with leather sofas and smoked

mirror, was the interior interpretation of the power suits of the Eighties. This has morphed into today's minimalism and modernism. The great furniture classics from Charles and Ray Eames, Arne Jacobsen, Mies van der Rohe and Gio Ponti have, of course, endured these changes and have influenced the younger design talents of Philippe Starck, Ron Arad, Jasper Morrison and the Bouroullec brothers.

The growth of the media has had a huge effect on everybody's aspirations – from the solitary supremacy of Fanny Craddock and Percy Thrower we now have dozens of foodies, chefs, stylists and garden designers vying for TV airtime. And as British magazines and newspapers picked up on the fact that people were interested in interiors, sporadic features gave way to dedicated sections, and then to a large number of mainstream titles devoted to the home. Lifestyle has become big business – there appears to be an unquenchable appetite for knowing how to arrange flowers, make curtains, cook a tagine, plant a border, host a party and tile a bathroom.

Going to restaurants, once considered to be a special occasion, has become part of everyday life. So many of us sit in front of a screen all day, and often go home to another screen in the evenings; a night out in a restaurant with friends is a way to catch up with human contact. Our drinking habits have altered too. Travel to the Continent has shown that wine is very *ordinaire* and has become part of the staple, middle-class meal. Women are drinking more. From a genteel sherry favoured by ladies in the Fifties, today's ladettes can match the lads pint for pint.

People started to need, want and be able to afford cars. In the Fifties the best mode of transport for the young man about town was a Vespa scooter or a Fiat – today it's got to be something with four-wheel drive, GTI and ESP. Although such is road congestion that scooter bicycles and tiny cars are finding favour once more.

These changes in style and taste have covered every aspect of our lives – how we live, what we eat, where we work, how we spend our time and money, how we travel and how we entertain ourselves. Has all this change been for the better? To most people in post-war Britain, function was more important than form. Since the arrival of central heating and a more comfortable lifestyle, design has had its chance to shine. Change is not necessarily always for the better, but at least in 2002 we have the luxury of choice.

Sir Terence Conran is founder of the Design Museum

When life brightened up

Britain began to enjoy itself in the Sixties. Art, fashion and music flourished. The Beatles were the nation's troubadours. Abroad, as colonies gained independence and the Commonwealth was being forged, Prime Minister Harold Macmillan spoke in 1960 of the "wind of change" sweeping through Africa

Dressed for the rain *on the moors near Balmoral (left) in the summer of 1960, the Queen was photographed off-duty – a picture that was a sign of the less formal times.*

Dressed for the sea *in a Royal Navy admiral's boat cloak (right), this romanticised official portrait by Cecil Beaton in 1968 was widely praised in the newspapers. "There have been so many pictures of the Queen in tiaras and Orders and crinoline that I felt I must do something different," he said.*

What the Queen sees. *A rare picture from the Queen's point of view (below), as people peer in at her car windows during a tour of Somerset in June 1966. A month later, England were victorious in the World Cup, beating Germany 4-2 at Wembley, and Time magazine, in a cover story about "Swinging London", wrote that it was "the city of the decade".*

On tour in India and Pakistan in January 1961, the Queen rode into **Jaipur** (top left) on the Maharajah of Jaipur's elephant and drove into **Rawalpindi** (above) in President Ayub Khan's high-fins Cadillac. In **Calcutta** (left) as if proving that this was the world's most populous democracy, huge crowds turned out.

Meanwhile, the Russians were preparing a different form of transport, and in April 27-year-old Yuri Gagarin orbited the earth at a height of 190 miles for 108 minutes to become the first man in space. In June, the Queen gave a lunch at the palace for him. When Gagarin drove through London in an open car, traffic came to a standstill as thousands thronged the streets to see him. But Cold War hostilities continued. East Germany built a 30-mile long wall across Berlin almost overnight on 13 August 1961, to stop the exodus of its citizens to the West.

"I... do become your liege man *of life and limb"*
was the oath of loyalty Prince Charles made to the
Queen at his investiture as Prince of Wales (right) in
Caernarfon Castle in July 1969. In the same year 'Royal
Family', a BBC film about a year in the life of the Queen,
went out to 125 countries and was seen by more people
than any other documentary ever made.

"Arise, Sir Francis" *The Queen knighted 65-year-old*
Francis Chichester (below), first man to sail around the
world singlehanded, in July 1967. She went to Greenwich
to knight him in the same place and with the same
sword with which Queen Elizabeth I had knighted
Sir Francis Drake after his circumnavigation of the
world in the Golden Hinde in 1580.

Prince Andrew, *the Queen's third child, was born on*
19 February 1960. This portrait of mother and baby
(far right) was taken by Cecil Beaton.

The birth of British couture By Colin McDowell

As Princess Elizabeth married in November 1947, the fashion world was still reeling from the New Look bombshell recently dropped by Christian Dior. The New Look had been such a success that it made everything else seem old-fashioned, but it presented a problem in Britain and particularly to the Palace. Clothing was still rationed. Not even a princess had enough clothing coupons for a New Look trousseau, which was all about full skirts sweeping down to the ankles. Donations of coupons flooded into the Palace which were all graciously returned, and the Board of Trade gave the Princess special dispensation – after all, how could the country allow a future queen to go on her honeymoon looking dowdy?

Princess Elizabeth was considered a style leader for her generation, a position she maintained during the early years of her reign. The Fifties were the last decade when elegance reigned unquestioned. Most young women dressed like their mothers in formal suits and 'princess' line coats.

Fashion originated in Paris, although London had its own strong couture group, led by the Queen's dressmakers Norman Hartnell and Hardy Amies. It was a time of formal evening wear and both couturiers produced spectacular romantic evening gowns for the Queen. Life was duller for ordinary young women. There was little in fashion specifically geared to them until the early Sixties when, to everyone's surprise, fashion's centre of gravity swung from Paris to London.

'Swinging London' broke all the rules and put young women in the fashion driving seat for the first time in history. London had the best of everything and the world couldn't wait to grab it. Fashion was dominated by Mary Quant and the King's Road; photography centred on David Bailey and Terence Donovan; and for hair, there was only one man – Vidal Sassoon. Highly irreverent, the young changed society's attitudes overnight. Everyone longed to look sexy – a completely new word in the fashion vocabulary.

The hedonistic helter-skelter had to slow down. During the Seventies, fashion took on the hippy look, with big-haired men in crushed velvet jeans and girls wearing gypsy waistcoats and milkmaid skirts. It was the decade of denims and flares, with wide inserts of floral prints below the knees. But some still longed for glamour, personified by Jerry Hall and the Biba look – a campy return to the 'Orient Express' Thirties elegance.

As the Seventies swung into the Eighties, a darker side of fashion began to appear. Punk gave rise to Goths, complete with spiky hair in dayglow shades, body piercing and tattoos. It was the beginning of the reign of black. The monotony was relieved by New Romanticism, when the boys began to rival the girls by wearing make-up and jewellery of an extravagance not seen since the days of Charles I.

But the real thing about the Eighties was the rise of the British designer on the world fashion stage. Important figures had emerged earlier of course with Ossie Clark, Zandra Rhodes and Jean Muir. But this was a time when designers such as Jasper Conran and Bruce Oldfield were giving the Princess of Wales an unprecedented royal fashion presence.

All paled into insignificance when compared with Vivienne Westwood, twentieth-century fashion's great maverick. Entirely untrained she made her name working with Malcolm McLaren creating outrageous twists on punk before moving into her own world of romantic and sexually specific variations on history in general and royalty in particular.

Westwood's influence on fashion in the early Nineties was considerable. Fashion students followed her example in turning their back on shoulder pads, logos and high-voltage hair. They were stalking something much more visceral.

By the mid-Nineties, the products of British art schools ruled the world. Led by John Galliano, closely followed by Alexander McQueen and Stella McCartney, they re-wrote the fashion story in a brilliant mixture of rock-chick raunchiness, eclectic ethnic romanticism, and hard-edged aggression which totally defined female fashion for the new millennium. Their influence has been immense and is still continuing, a fashion fact acknowledged by the Queen herself in 2001 when she made John Galliano a Commander of the British Empire. I like to think that it was also Her Majesty's own way of saying that, although protocol (and her age!) may have precluded her from following many of the exciting developments which have made British fashion such a force during her reign, she is aware of the achievements of London fashion and takes pride in them.

Colin McDowell is a fashion historian and critic for The Sunday Times

Lady Helen Taylor, *a UK ambassador for Armani (above) wears an Armani Collezioni pinstriped suit in 2002.*

Princess Diana *wearing an evening gown (right) by a favourite designer, Catherine Walker.*

Princess Margaret *(left), a fashion icon of the Fifties and Sixties.*

Viscountess Serena Linley *(top) at Ascot in Hervé Léger.* **Lady Sarah Chatto** *(right) attends the wedding of her brother Viscount Linley.*

On the move in her busy schedule during the Sixties (top), the Queen saw for herself the bleak reality of the Cold War on a visit to the **Berlin Wall** with Prince Philip in 1965. And in the **Shetlands** in 1960 (left), Prince Philip drove her around in one of the Royal Mail vans that double as buses for the islanders. Opening the new **Victoria Line** (below) in 1969, the Queen rode in the driver's cab of a London Underground train.

Staying home *in 1967, the Queen was photographed informally at Balmoral for The Observer Magazine. It was the first time the photographer, David Montgomery, had taken any royal portraits. "I thought I would just let the Queen decide where she would like to be photographed. She said near the fire – then just went over and sat down beside it. The corgis followed her and plonked themselves down."*

The State Funeral of Sir Winston Churchill (left) was attended by the royal family at St Paul's Cathedral. Among the distinguished mourners, General de Gaulle, President of France (second left, middle row), came to pay his last respects to his wartime comrade-in-arms. Sir Winston died, aged 90, in January 1965 and his flag-draped coffin was carried on a naval gun-carriage through the streets of London lined with thousands of onlookers.

Another world leader was remembered at Runnymede in 1965 (above). On the meadow where Magna Carta was signed, the Queen greeted Mrs Jacqueline Kennedy, her two children, John Jnr. and Caroline, and her brother-in-law, Senator Robert Kennedy, when she unveiled a memorial to US President John F Kennedy, who had been assassinated in 1963.

A minute's silence (below) beside the wreckage of the village school at Aberfan in South Wales, buried by a colliery slag heap which slid down a mountainside in October 1966, killing 144 people, most of them children.

Dancing at the
Ghillies Ball at
Balmoral with
Prince Philip.

50 years of Britpop

by Jools Holland

THE 2ND JUNE 1952 signalled the beginning of many new things. The young Queen Elizabeth was to rule over the most peaceful and prosperous 50 years we have known, and we were on the brink of exciting cultural changes, especially in popular music.

In 1952 some of us were still enjoying the big bands or listening to the great Vera Lynn or Gracie Fields, we might spend an evening at the Music Hall or a sing song at the piano, but a new style was coming which would be picked up by some young musicians who would go on to influence the world. In London Chris Barber, Alexis Korner, Cyril Davis and Humphrey Lyttleton were boogieing to American jazz and blues. They invented their own take on it which paved the way for British blues performers like the Rolling Stones, Eric Clapton and Long John Baldry.

Until the late Fifties our main influence was America: we took their sounds and made them our own. Lonnie Donegan gave us skiffle music which could be played on homemade instruments, while Rory and Alex McEwan mixed Leadbelly with Scottish and Irish folk music influencing musicians, including Van Morrison.

By the end of the Fifties we had given birth to our own pop stars – good looking as well as talented. Joe Brown was an amazing singer and guitarist, and Cliff Richard was gifted with a brilliant voice. My grandfather, Percy Holland, took my teenage aunt to see young Cliff perform. He waited outside the theatre in his official-looking Wolseley saloon. A girl asked what he was doing and, in a lightning display of Holland humour, he told them he was Cliff's driver. A hoard of teenage girls, excited by this, pushed his car on its side whilst screaming "we love Cliff".

This mania was just the tip of the iceberg. In the early 1960s Liverpool gave us a musical force which was to change the world of popular music forever. They were, and remain, one of the few groups where we all know all of their names. John, Paul, George and Ringo were The Beatles. Unlike stars that came before them, they wrote all their own songs which were some of the greatest of the 20th century.

As the Sixties continued, an extraordinary amount of talent flourished – The Who, the Yardbirds, the Kinks, Cream, Pink Floyd, Manfred Mann – who would define pop music at home and abroad. The Rolling Stones were the greatest rock and roll group and remain the most successful touring act in the world. It was a time when many great singers shone in our musical landscape. Dusty Springfield, Petula Clark, Cilla Black, Lulu were all adored. It's hard to imagine anything more exciting than seeing a young Tom Jones belting out rock and roll in the tough clubs of the Welsh valleys where he began.

The Seventies dawned, and musically we were unstoppable. The world was given heavy metal by Led Zeppelin, Deep Purple and Black Sabbath. ELO popularised the orchestral sound, T-Rex reinvented the boogie, Status Quo were rocking all over the world and a young David Bowie lit up the scene. We heard the unique voices of Rod Stewart and Bryan Ferry, and the extraordinary pianist and songwriter Elton John conquered the world. Queen did the same. At the end of the decade, a whole new wave of bands appeared to excite our palate. The Sex Pistols, The Clash, Squeeze, U2, The Jam, The Police and Dire Straits are just a handful who were to be successful in America and beyond.

The Fifties and Sixties saw a large influx of Jamaicans, who brought with them their own wonderful sound. By the Eighties this influence was manifesting itself with groups like Selector, Madness and The Specials. First and second generation musicians such as Rico Rodriguez, Ruby Turner and Eddie Grant became a major part of British music. Musical poets Elvis Costello, Robert Wyatt and Ian Dury emerged. As we sped through the decade, you could walk into a bar or club in any city on earth and hear Duran Duran, Pet Shop Boys, Eurythmics or Phil Collins.

As the Nineties unfurled we still had great singers – Mick Hucknall and Paul Weller touched our emotions. In a renaissance of British pop music, Blur, Oasis and Pulp reinvented the British pop song. Jamiroquai had their own take on funk, there was an explosion of dance music led by Fat Boy Slim and the Prodigy, the Spice Girls brought back teen mania and Lord Lloyd-Webber continued to be a worldwide success with his musicals.

The new century dawned with Radiohead, Travis, Robbie Williams and Dido making an impression. Gabrielle, Cerys Matthews, Beverley Knight and Mica Paris soothed our souls with their voices. The greats – Eric Clapton, U2, Paul McCartney, Sting and Elton John – were at their peak.

It is impossible here to mention all the great talent that has come from Britain. What remains is to ask what our musical future holds. In the last 50 years we have produced amazing talent and led the world. I believe all the people I have mentioned loved what they played, played what they loved and loved the people they played to. I am confident that young talent will continue to do this. Then we will have another 50 years of wonderful music. And, I hope, another 50 years of peace and prosperity.

Jools Holland is a musician and broadcaster

The Fab Four
with their MBEs

A decade with a silver lining

The dancing years of the Sixties were over. This was a decade of anxiety and debt. Inflation soared. Terrorism, at home and abroad, became a fact of life. Though the Vietnam war ended, another war broke out in the Middle East, causing oil shortages in the West. The Queen celebrated her silver wedding anniversary, and street parties for her Silver Jubilee were a bright interlude in an anxious, edgy decade

Yorkshire miners gathered *around the Queen before she went underground at Silverwood Colliery, South Yorkshire, in 1975 (above). Her safety attire caused great excitement in the national press, as if a new fashion trend had been launched – the Daily Mail headlining its picture "The Queen of the Coalface". Later, the National Coal Board used the picture in a safety pamphlet, with the slogan 'Follow Her Majesty's example – wear safety clothing'. Silverwood, known then as a long-life mine, often produced more than a million tons of coal a year, but as alternative sources of energy became available it was shut down in 1994. The pay freeze of 5 per cent imposed by the Government to curb inflation – which reached 24 per cent in 1975 – caused a miners' strike in the winter of 1973-4. Coal shortages at power stations resulted in a three-day working week, a general election and the fall of Edward Heath's Government.*

At Balmoral *in 1972, the Queen and Prince Philip celebrated their Silver Wedding Anniversary, and posed for this portrait by Patrick Lichfield.*

Laughs all round, *as the Queen stands beside Prince Philip's four-in-hand carriage (above), listening to his account of an event at the Royal Windsor Horse Show in 1978, and as she jumps ashore from a floating jetty in Turkey in 1971 (below).*

Government red boxes *follow the Queen wherever she goes. On board Britannia in 1972 (below) she studies official documents, attended by her private secretary, Sir Martin Charteris. In his recent biography 'Royal', Robert Lacey writes: "For long hours every week she sits stolidly reading, annotating and signing the documents that come into her boxes". Another biographer, Sarah Bradford, reveals in 'Elizabeth' that it's a mistake for ministers to think that the Queen might have skimped her work. In 1955 Prime Minister Anthony Eden and Colonial Secretary Alan Lennox-Boyd were surprised by the extent of her knowledge of the Commonwealth. Before sending one of his memoranda to the Palace, Lennox-Boyd was anxious about a detail concerning the grazing rights of Somali tribesmen; Eden thought the Queen might not ask, or even know about the question – but she did.*

Cameras, action! *Schoolchildren on a history project were given special permission for this close-up position at a doorway of Westminster Abbey as the Queen, wearing the robes of the Order of the Bath, left an installation service for Knights of the Bath in October 1972. A month later, the Queen was at Westminster Abbey with Prince Philip, for a service of thanksgiving on their silver wedding anniversary. At lunch afterwards in the City of London Guildhall, the Queen said, "I think everybody will concede that on this of all days I should begin my speech: 'My husband and I'." This was the year in which the Northern Ireland parliament was dissolved and direct rule from Westminster imposed after the weeks of violence following 'Bloody Sunday' in January. Thirteen people were killed and 17 wounded when British soldiers opened fire on a civil rights demonstration in Londonderry. In the summer of the same year, Black September terrorists broke into the athletes' village at the Munich Olympics, took Israeli competitors hostage and killed 11 of them when a rescue attempt failed.*

A force for good

by Richard Holmes

BRITAIN'S ARMED FORCES have seen major changes between Her Majesty's accession and her Golden Jubilee. Figures do not tell the whole story but are in themselves striking. In 1952 there were some 932,000 Regular personnel in the services, and their reserves – regular and volunteer – were large, with a Territorial Army consisting of fully-equipped divisions. Defence, consuming some 10 per cent of Gross Domestic Product (GDP), was the largest single item of Government expenditure. By 2000 there were just fewer than 208,000 Regulars, the Territorial Army numbered around 42,000, and defence absorbed 2.5 per cent of GDP, well below social security, health and education. The Spithead review of 1953 featured almost 200 warships, about four times more than the Royal Navy currently possesses. Then the British Army of the Rhine contained four divisions: now there is a single armoured division based in Germany.

Appearances reinforce statistics. In 1952 National Service, conscription for young men, was a feature of national life. Service personnel routinely wore uniform, and were a well-understood part of a nation which had just emerged from major war. Dockyards, shore establishments and airfields were numerous, and county regiments, still un-amalgamated, were based in the great redbrick Victorian barracks in county towns. Although the services still enjoy a wide public approval, the level of public understanding of the armed forces has declined.

Across the period, Britain has moved from garrisoning an empire and facing a major land threat in Europe to maintaining expeditionary forces which are primarily home-based. In 1952 Britain retained the trappings of world power, and was adjusting to the Cold War. In February of that year, NATO's 'Lisbon Goals' called for conventional force levels to match the scale of the threat posed by Russia and her allies, but Prime Minister Winston Churchill admitted that rearmament on this scale was "utterly beyond our economic capacity to bear". British troops were actively engaged in operations: there were, for example, 25,000 British and another 10,000 Gurkha soldiers in Malaya, and the Mau Mau insurgency in Kenya, which began in 1952, was soon to absorb 35,000 troops and local forces.

The imbalance between commitments and resources was emphasised in the 1952 Global Strategy Paper which suggested that nuclear deterrence should become the central tenet of British defence policy – albeit as "a contribution to the Allied deterrent" – and the first British atomic bomb was tested in October that year. The Duncan Sandys defence review of 1957 recommended "a nuclear deterrent of Britain's own". It saw the prime purpose of defence as "to prevent war rather than prepare for it", and to achieve this would "threaten retaliation with nuclear weapons". Nuclear strength would be paralleled by conventional reductions: the forces were to be reduced from 690,000 to 375,000, and National Service was to end in 1960.

Nuclear deterrence remained a cornerstone of defence policy, although there was often a tension between policy and practice, which required conventional forces for a wide variety of tasks. These included a number of small 'brushfire wars' across the world, helping maintain security in Northern Ireland, recapturing the Falklands in 1982 and furnishing an armoured division to the coalition which defeated Saddam Hussein in 1990-91.

In 1998 the Labour Government published its Strategic Defence Review which sought to establish policy-led defence planning, against a background of international engagement and a desire for Britain to act as a "force for good" in the world. The nuclear deterrent was retained, and the expeditionary character of Britain's armed forces was underlined. They would need to be able to conduct "frequent, often simultaneous and sometimes prolonged" operations overseas. In early 2002 the SDR New Chapter, a public discussion paper, outlined ways in which the 11 September terrorist attack on the USA might affect British defence policy, though it did not seem to presage radical change.

As the nation celebrates the Jubilee it can applaud the achievements of the armed forces. They are indeed a force for good in the world, with recent successes in the Balkans, East Timor and Sierra Leone. They have been generally successful in meeting changing social demands: they tolerate homosexuality, have taken great strides towards obliterating racism, and have thrown a growing number of posts open to women. Veterans of the 1950s would be struck by the absence of 'bull' and obtrusive discipline.

While doctrine can be taught and weapons can be bought, men and women prepared to risk their lives are the bedrock on which successful armed forces stand: attracting and retaining people who feel valued and valuable, is fundamentally important. This was true in 1952, and it is just as true today.

Professor Richard Holmes is a military historian and broadcaster

The retiring Prime Minister,
Harold Wilson, greeting the Queen at
10 Downing Street (above) as she arrived
for his farewell dinner on 5 April 1976.

Ceremonial duties. The Queen takes
the salute (left) during Trooping the
Colour in 1979, the annual official
celebration of her birthday.

The President of Yugoslavia,
Marshal Tito, and his wife, welcoming
the Queen to Belgrade, (below) when
she made a State Visit in 1972 – the
first by a reigning monarch to a
Communist country.

Silver Wedding family gathering, *photographed by the Queen's cousin, Patrick Lichfield (the Earl of Lichfield) at Buckingham Palace in 1972, when the Queen and Prince Philip celebrated their silver wedding anniversary. Grouped around the Queen are, from left to right, seated: Princess Margaret; the Duchess of Kent, with Lord Nicholas Windsor on her lap; the Queen Mother; Princess Anne; Marina Ogilvy; Princess Alexandra. Children seated on floor, left to right: Lady Sarah Armstrong-Jones; Viscount Linley; Prince Edward; Lady Helen Windsor. Standing, left to right: Earl of Snowdon; the Duke of Kent; Prince Michael of Kent; Prince Philip; the Earl of St Andrews (eldest son of the Duke and Duchess of Kent); the Prince of Wales; Prince Andrew; Mr Angus Ogilvy, (husband of Princess Alexandra); James Ogilvy.*

51

The first-ever walkabout

*by the Queen (left) took place
on Jubilee Day, when after the
thanksgiving service at St Paul's,
she made her way through the
crowds between the cathedral
and the Mansion House.*

The Gold State Coach *in which the Queen rode to her coronation took her to St Paul's Cathedral for the service of thanksgiving on her Silver Jubilee Day. By 9am the crowds stood six deep along the route from the palace to the cathedral. The streets were awash with red, white and blue (right) and 'Liz Rules, OK!' was the slogan most frequently seen on badges, on banners and chalked on walls at the 12,000 street parties counted by Mass Observation throughout the country. It was all done, said royal biographer Robert Lacey, in a jubilee tradition dating back to George III: "The historic power of communal ritual proved as inspirational as ever". A Southampton woman wrote to the Mass Observation survey, "With the economic state of the country, people have been feeling a bit low, and this Silver Jubilee is just what people needed to cheer them up a bit".*

Taste of the times
by Prue Leith

Although the war had ended nearly eight years before, times were still tough when the Queen was crowned. Rationing did not end until the following year, and I remember the horrified silence that greeted my brother dropping our whole family's weekly egg ration (four eggs in a paper bag) onto a stone floor. My mother scooped them up.

Sweets were rationed too. Once, sorry for some prisoners of war digging a trench in the Edgware Road, I held out my bag of toffees for them each to take one. The first one took the whole bag. Never mind, said my mother, you'll get another bag next month, and they won't.

If the diet was dull, it was healthier than it has ever been since, with plenty of potatoes, bread and vegetables and precious little protein. Our steady progress to fattest nation in Europe began with the end of rationing in 1954.

Then followed a diverging path – increasing affluence for many in the Sixties meant foreign travel. The young Elizabeth David, who had spent the war in Greece and North Africa, had come home to the dreariness of post-war Britain and had longed for the smell of peppers and lemons, for the robust tastes of the warm south. She published *A Book of Mediterranean Food*, and even today, there is hardly a chef or a dedicated home-cook who does not trace their love of food, directly or indirectly to her. The adventurous were tempted to tackle moussaka, paella and spaghetti bolognaise, often served from the heated hostess trolley.

By the Seventies, supermarkets were ousting local shops with bulk buys and TV dinners. Frozen veg was now more popular than canned. By the Eighties, we'd learnt that olive oil was not just for soothing earache and we could buy ready-washed salad and chilled tiramisu. By the Nineties the supermarkets were selling fresh Indian curries, and by the end of the century the affluent customer did not need to cook at all.

Preparing food had been getting easier if you had the money. Food mixers, pressure cookers, automatic cookers and, above all, freezers made life simpler. By the boom-time Eighties the wealthy boasted designer kitchens, often with machines to make ice cream, pasta, bread and cappuccino. The less well-off bought crisps, pot snacks, frozen pizza

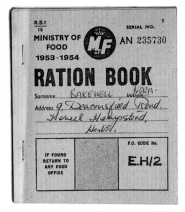

and biscuits. How many children today have a packet of crisps or sweets for breakfast? Not all kitchens have improved – once every household had an oven and a table for eating at. Today, if young mums cannot cook, what is the point of an oven? And if everyone eats ready-meals round the TV, why have a dining table?

Fifty years ago few people ate out. On weekdays pubs served up reheated steak pies and unappetising sandwiches, and there was no food at all on offer on Sundays. The Kardomah Coffee Bar offered a trendier venue for the young and Lyons Corner Houses offered a staid, even elegant, family outing. But their future was threatened by the spread of KFC and McDonalds in the Seventies which also hastened the decline of the traditional fish and chip and eel and pie shops.

For the upmarket customer, eating out in the Fifties and Sixties had meant white-clothed hotel restaurants with intimidating waiters serving predictable French food. But the old guard was challenged by restaurateurs like Robert Carrier and George Perry-Smith, unhampered by traditional hotel training.

In the Seventies, the nouvelle cuisine revolution encouraged chefs to experiment with new ingredients and to put the emphasis on quality, freshness and the look of the thing. But by the Eighties what had been innovative became gimmicky – "a little bit of decoration on a big white plate". Reaction came with "comfort food" – big portions of risotto, pasta, bangers and mash. By the end of the millennium, vegetarianism had ceased to be a novelty and it seemed like more meals were being eaten out of the home than in it.

And in this age of celebrity, food too has its stars. In the Fifties Fanny Craddock had riveted viewers as she cooked in full evening dress. Marguerite Patten's *Cookery in Colour* set the trend for illustrated cookbooks. In the Seventies Delia Smith arrived to show the nation how to cook, the Eighties brought ebullient Antony Worrall Thompson and the slurping Keith Floyd, swiftly followed by a chorus of extroverts, more concerned with entertainment than teaching us to cook.

By the Nineties, we were watching Gary Rhodes perform on the TV while we ate takeaways on the sofa. And the turn of the century has brought us the young Jamie Oliver, whose recipes, we are told, are actually followed, just like Delia's are. Are we back to really cooking again? Maybe there is still some hope for us yet.

Prue Leith, OBE is a chef, restaurateur and author

With flags and bunting *flying (left), children in Belfast enjoy a street party celebrating the Queen's Silver Jubilee in 1977.*

The good, the bad and the yuppie

In the 'Big Bang' City, the yuppie was born, and we laughed at our sudden 'loadsamoney' culture, but in a recent reappraisal of the Eighties, The Sunday Times said it was "a brutal decade in which high unemployment created ever-widening social divisions…" As well as the weddings of two of her sons, the decade also saw the Queen welcome home Prince Andrew from active service in the Falklands War

With this kiss, on the balcony of Buckingham Palace, the nation's fever over the marriage of Prince Charles to Lady Diana Spencer peaked in the summer of 1981. In the same summer there were riots and fires in deprived inner-city areas, the worst being at Toxteth, Liverpool and Brixton, London. Author Robert Lacey wrote: "News bulletins presented a bizarre combination of urban ghettos in flames alongside wedding dress speculation".

This official portrait was taken in 1985 (right), when the Queen was 59. Three years earlier she coped with the most bizarre episode of her reign: an intruder who was mentally disturbed broke into Buckingham Palace and reached her bedroom when Prince Philip was away. The Queen pressed an alarm bell and calmly made two telephone calls to the police, keeping the man talking until they arrived.

A tour and two armies: *the Queen saw the terracotta army in the tomb of the Emperor Qin Shihuang (left) while on her tour of China in 1986, and inspected an honour guard (below) of the People's Liberation Army in Beijing.*

President and Mrs Reagan *were hosts to the Queen and Prince Philip on their visit to America early in 1983. There was entertainment in Hollywood (near right) and at a White House banquet in Washington (far right), where the Queen amused the President with her speech.*

The US-UK 'special relationship' was put under strain in October that year when, perceiving a Cuban-backed threat to its security, America invaded Grenada, a Commonwealth island in the Caribbean, to quell an uprising in which the Prime Minister had been murdered. Mrs Thatcher was said to be "incandescent" on the telephone to President Reagan, and The Times reported that the Queen was not best pleased "at the notion that foreign powers may walk into member states of the Commonwealth without prior warning".

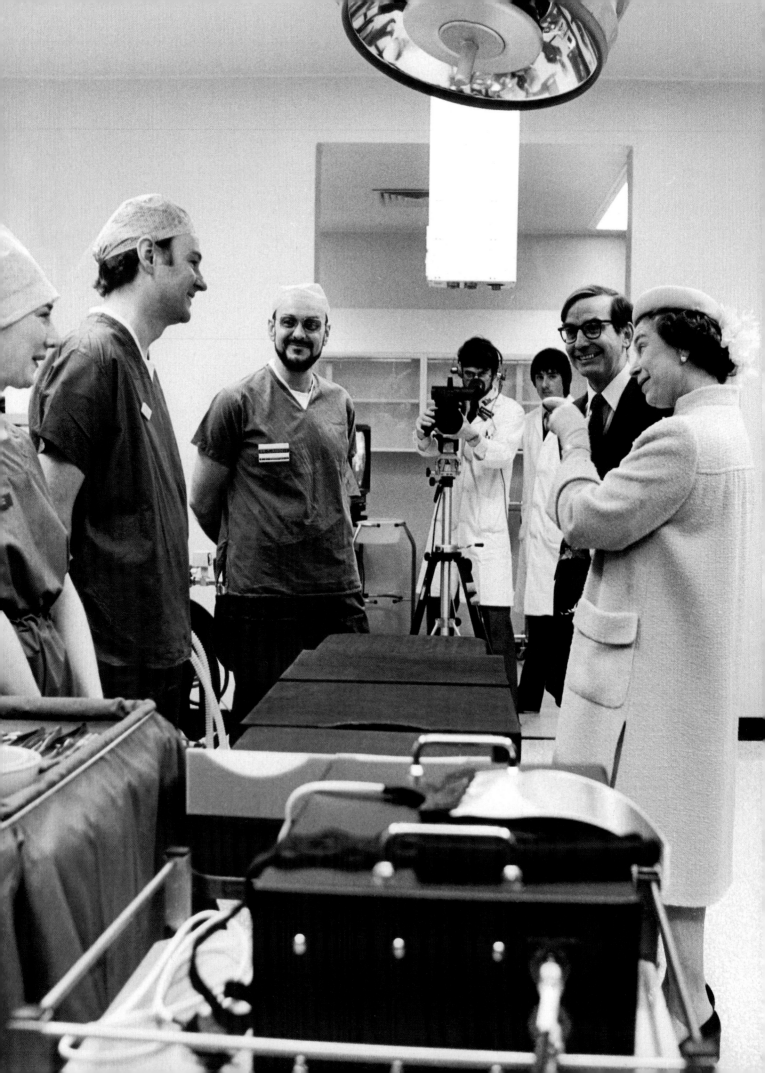

Talking about a revolution

by Heather Couper

Sitting in my old, heavily-beamed cottage, it seems that the 21st century is a long way off, as I gaze over miles of green English countryside. But it's due to a revolution that I have the freedom to live here, high in the Chiltern Hills – a revolution in information and electronics.

When the Queen acceded to the throne, the information explosion hadn't even been predicted. Computers were the size of buses, and phoning abroad was a tricky business. Now I can e-mail anywhere in the world in an instant. If I want to check a fact, I go into a search engine on the internet. When a radio station wants an interview, I re-route my ISDN telephone line – which usually brings the internet into my computer – to a mixer. To me, this is one of the greatest advances in science and technology that has taken place since 1952. And there have been countless others. Fifty years ago, Britain was a very different place; one that our Victorian and even Georgian ancestors would have recognized. People lived life much as they had in the past.

In fact, a lot of people hanker after those "good old days", but in many respects they are an illusion. Advances in medical science over the past 50 years have meant that we are living longer, and in many cases, more healthily. We're learning to control disease. And we are getting a better understanding of how life itself works. The unravelling of the structure of DNA – the molecule responsible for heredity – in Britain in 1953 has led to a revolution in genetics that continues unabated to this day. Dolly, the cloned sheep, is a much-loved British institution.

With these controversial advances comes a need for greater responsibility. All of us need to be involved in debate about what is ethical and what is not. This has echoes of issues concerning our industrial growth over the past 50 years, when we realised that some practices were causing pollution. Industry started to police itself – and now we are all more environmentally aware.

Part of the reason for our heightened concern for the environment of both our nation and our planet is because we can accurately monitor changes from space. From the vantage-point of satellites – many built in Britain – we can now see the devastation to the rain forests, or industrial pollution in the Eastern Bloc, as it happens. Satellites have brought many far-reaching changes into our daily lives. Instant communications, a choice of hundreds of television channels and more accurate weather forecasts are all the result of a host of satellites patrolling the high frontier.

Space is, of course, another major breakthrough of the past 50 years. When England's Astronomer Royal heard rumours that Russia had launched Sputnik in 1957, he dismissed them as "utter bilge". What would he have thought, just 12 years later, when men were walking on the Moon? Today, we have sent spaceprobes to every planet of our Solar System except distant Pluto; around 400 people have flown in space; and we're on the dawn of space tourism, when anyone with the necessary money will be able to see the Blue Planet from orbit.

There will be places where we can never go, but that hasn't stopped astronomers from performing some exquisite hands-off detective work. During my lifetime, which virtually coincides with the Queen's reign, I have seen a breakthrough in our knowledge of the cosmos as dramatic as when Galileo first pointed a telescope to the heavens.

Thanks to cutting-edge technologies, new windows on the Universe have opened up. Radio astronomy, as exemplified by the huge telescopes at Jodrell Bank and Cambridge, is one of the British-driven initiatives which look at the cosmos that light does not reveal. So too, does X-ray astronomy – also pioneered in Britain – which seeks out cosmic violators such as black holes and exploding stars. Over the past 50 years, British astronomers have helped build up a picture of the way our Universe works – and these discoveries are being used by physicists to build up a description of it and of what makes it tick.

In the last five decades, we have all come a long, long way. We have passed through some of the biggest changes in our values and perceptions that human beings may ever be required to undertake. But when the dust has cleared, I hope that we will see the true contribution of science and technology to our lives. In the end, it has provided us with the greatest perspective of all – of who we are and where we are in the vast cosmos we inhabit.

Dr Heather Couper is a broadcaster and writer on astronomy and science

Humour in the theatre *as the Queen meets surgeons (left) after opening a new wing of the London Hospital, in the East End, in 1982.*

The horse world, *wrote biographer Ben Pimlott, is central to the Queen's life. One fellow enthusiast, President Ronald Reagan, rode out with the Queen in Windsor Great Park (above) on a visit to Britain in 1982. And at the Royal Windsor Horse Show (right, in 1985) the Queen can enjoy this world in which she is an acknowledged expert. She has owned racehorses since 1949 and in 1957 became leading winner-owner in Britain for the second time. She has won all the flat racing classics, except the Derby. But as racing and horse breeding have become a highly competitive global business, the Queen's racing stable of just 20 mares is modest by comparison with the big players.*

The Queen's riding skills *kept her horse, Burmese, under control when six blank shots were fired at her in the Mall (left) as she rode to the Trooping the Colour in June 1981. A 17-year-old youth was arrested and later sentenced to two years' imprisonment. The black mare shied not at the shots but because the Household Cavalry moved in suddenly to protect the Queen. She explained to her staff afterwards: "Burmese felt that the Household Cavalry was going to attack me, so she attacked them first".*

Monarch of the mudmen, *Papua, New Guinea, 1980. The Queen, with Prince Philip, Princess Anne and her first husband, Captain Mark Phillips, greeted by the Asaro tribe (above), who cover their faces in mud masks to commemorate an ancient tribal victory. The Papuans are unique in having chosen the Queen to become their monarch. The country was never part of the British Empire but was governed under an Australian mandate until 1973, when it was given independence. Two years later they joined the Commonwealth and invited the Queen to be head of state. When Sir Martin Charteris, the Queen's private secretary, asked why, he was told 'Because they like her because she's been there. Second, because they want someone who will be above local squabbles.'*

In the South Pacific, *the Queen and Prince Philip are carried through the streets by islanders (top) in the Commonwealth archipelago of Tuvalu in 1982.*

The revered Mother Teresa, *receiving the Order of Merit (above) from the Queen in India in 1983.*

Pope John Paul II *leaving Buckingham Palace (left) during a visit to Britain in 1982.*

The view from '52

by Mark Lawson

THE DATE ON WHICH A REIGN BEGINS is arbitrary – decided by medical rather than cultural history – but, in retrospect, the year 1952 does reveal the patterns of re-arrangement.

In one area of culture, the change was specifically created by the constitutional movement. The funeral of the King and the subsequent coronation of the Queen resulted in the first mass purchase of television sets. An estimated 50,000 viewers (restricted to the London area) had watched the coronation of George VI; more than 20 million would see the crown being placed on his daughter's head after the new monarch over-ruled Prime Minister Winston Churchill and admitted cameras to the

Abbey. If the legend is true that she agreed to TV's presence in order to allow the house-bound Queen Mary to view the ceremony, then the most powerful mass medium in British history owes its start to a small act of family kindness.

Those 1952-53 television schedules reveal many prototypes of shows made today. Only two programmes – *Panorama* and *Bill and Ben The Flowerpot Men* – are still broadcast but the genres are very recognisable. The game-show was represented by *What's My Line?* and *Animal, Vegetable, Mineral?*. Philip Harben was ancestor-chef to the Delias, Jamies and Nigellas of today. The first-ever television thriller series – Francis Durbridge's *The Broken Horseshoe* – also laid down the DNA which would spawn millions of similar episodes.

Television – like all art-forms of the period – was very decorous. There was genuine outrage, rather than the tabloid-faked kind of today, when Richard Dimbleby was heard to swear on air. But 1952 sees the serious beginnings of the modernising and liberalising which would lead, five decades later, to an artist winning the Turner Prize for putting out the lights. Indeed, the modernist work which most outraged conservatives until Martin Creed's *The Lights Going On And Off* – John Cage's composition *4' 33"*, which consists of an orchestra sitting completely silent for that length of time – was premiered in 1952, giving the date a

neatness as a border-post between the old and new in culture.

From four and half minutes of silence to three minutes of loud noise: pop music – now a multi-billion dollar industry – was effectively invented by two breakthroughs of the time. Both the concept and the phrase "rock 'n' roll" were given general currency after the American DJ Alan Freed started to play black music on his programme. In November of 1952, the first pop singles chart was published in Britain.

The biggest hit film felt innocent enough – Gene Kelly in *Singin' In The Rain* – although even that film has a slightly knowing tone, sending up the genre of the musical: the famous splash-dance has no relevance to the plot. Spookily, one of the successes of that time, as of this, was *Moulin Rouge*. A comparison between John Huston's version then and Baz Luhrmann's now reveals the vast technical developments in filming and editing which have transformed cinema. Other films actually look transitional. Charlie Chaplin released his strangest work, *Limelight*, a farewell to the London and the entertainment business of his past, and British film buffs could also see Kurosawa's *Rashomon*, one of the first Japanese works to open in the West, its multiple storylines influencing numerous movies.

In literature, Evelyn Waugh published *Men At Arms*, beginning his *Sword Of Honour* trilogy, and the publication of Dylan Thomas's best-selling *Collected Poems* established a popularity which would be romantically solidified by his drinker's death the next year. Yet, setting the trend in writing for the next five decades, British authors were over-shadowed by publications from the big Americans: Hemingway's *The Old Man And The Sea*, Steinbeck's *East Of Eden* and Ralph Ellison's *Invisible Man*.

British theatre during this period offers, in one sense, an astonishing impression of continuity because one play which opened in 1952 – Agatha Christie's *The Mousetrap* – is still running. This consistency, however, is an illusion because the year can now be seen as one of drama's biggest hinge-dates.

In Paris, an Irishman, Samuel Beckett, wrote, in French, a play called *En Attendant Godot*. It soon after came to London, anglicised by him as *Waiting For Godot* and changed British dramatists' idea of what a play could be. Beckett's repetitive dialogue, retrieval of cliché, aimless action and major characters who never appear on stage rapidly inspired two young playwrights, Harold Pinter and Tom Stoppard, who came to dominate post-war British drama.

The release of surrealism into British theatre was another of the liberations from tradition – of form, language, content – which mark the culture of Elizabeth II's reign. Through a combination of coincidence and calculation on the part of artists, the accession began a period of cultural lèse-majesté.

Mark Lawson is a writer and broadcaster specialising in the arts

On the set of 'Coronation Street': *the Queen enjoys a visit t
Granada Studios in Manchester (right) in 1982, where she me
members of the cast outside Alf Roberts' corner shop*

The Cold War thaws and apartheid ends

After the fall of the Berlin Wall in 1989, the thaw in the Cold War continued and the Nineties began optimistically. In South Africa, Nelson Mandela was released after 27 years in jail, starting the process that led to his election as President, the end of apartheid and the return of the country to the Commonwealth

Mrs Margaret Thatcher *(above with the Queen at a Government reception) ended her tenure as Prime Minister, after 11 years in office, in November 1990.*

President Boris Yeltsin, *Russia's first democratically elected head of state, invited the Queen to Russia in 1994 and she and Prince Philip (right) were shown around Red Square by members of the Russian government. The Queen presented a delicate crystal chest of drawers, containing seeds specially harvested from the Buckingham Palace gardens, to Mrs Yeltsin, who is a keen gardener. Mr Yeltsin's gift to the Queen was an album of rare photographs, letters and documents of the last Tsar and his family, in which Prince Philip was able to point out to the Queen pictures of his Tsarist ancestors.*

The Queen at 70 – *this official portrait (far right) was released in 1996 to mark her 70th birthday.*

"She is devastated," *Prince Andrew, Duke of York, told a press conference after the Queen saw the damage (left), caused by a fire at her childhood home, Windsor Castle. Prince Andrew organised the rescue of all the paintings except one as the flames roared through the north-east corner of the castle on 20 November 1992, causing damage that would cost £37 million to repair. St George's Hall, nine state apartments and 100 other rooms were destroyed or badly damaged. Two days later, in a speech (far left) at a lunch given by the City of London to celebrate 40 years of her reign, the Queen said: "Nineteen ninety two is not a year I shall look back on with undiluted pleasure," and went on to describe it as "an annus horribilis". Apart from the Windsor fire, there had been the legal separation of the Duke and Duchess of York in March, and in April the divorce of the Princess Royal and Captain Mark Phillips. The following month, Buckingham Palace announced the separation of the Prince and Princess of Wales.*

The sailor Prince *pauses reflectively with the Queen beside the grave of a seaman killed during the D-Day landings in Normandy in 1944. The Second World War was a formative experience for the Queen and Prince Philip, and as part of the commemorative celebrations for the 50th anniversary of D-Day, they visited this cemetery maintained by the British and Commonwealth War Graves Commission at Bayeux.*

The electrician President, *Lech Walesa of Poland, rides in procession with the Queen (below) on his state visit to Britain in 1991. Mr Walesa – and the whole of Eastern Europe – had come a long way in the struggle which dismantled the Iron Curtain in 1989-90. The man from the Gdansk shipyard, whose Solidarity movement toppled Poland's Communist government in 1990, was a guest of the Queen at Windsor Castle. Before leaving Britain he gave a state banquet for the Queen at Claridge's in London.*

Passing on the baton

by Frank Keating

During her reign the Queen has seen British sport develop from an uncomplicated, homely ritual sponsored by fun, to a multinational, global industry sponsored, it so often seems, by opportunism and avarice. Yet the intrinsic appeal of sport, and its myriad benefits and glories, continues to throw up dramas and heroes perhaps unmatched by any other area of creative activity.

Then, top-drawer British sport was played by either gifted amateurs taking out a year or two to perform stirring deeds before returning, content, to the real world, or talented professionals who caught a bus to the ground with – and earned no more than – those in the vast throng which turned up to applaud them. The excellence inspired ecstatic local fervour or, sometimes, collective national passion. But that was as far as it went.

Now it is part of a frenetic worldwide free market, garlanded with advertising and endorsement contracts, in which its most successful performers have become universally lionised cultural icons who are among the most recognisable (and wealthy) celebrities on the planet. If TV, as many would say, has been the most dominant secular missionary of the half century, then sport has been its acolyte and blood brother.

Pioneer viewers saw the monarch give football's folk-hero Stanley Matthews his Cup Winners' Medal at Wembley, in the first televised Cup Final four weeks before her coronation. Then, just over 10 per cent of households had a TV. Thirteen years later when she presented the World Cup to Bobby Moore from the same balcony, fewer than 10 per cent were without one.

By nice fluke, when the young monarch ushered in her bonny new Elizabethan era of zestful expectation, a new generation of callow sportsmen was capturing imaginations. In the summer of 1952, 17-year-old Lester Piggott was second in the Derby; the two cricketers who were to define the game's future, 21-year-old Fred Trueman and, a year older, Peter May, played in a Test match together for the first time, and the dashing driver Stirling Moss, also 22, won his first motor race abroad.

Two other sporting markers for history were laid down that year — a first Football League championship since 1911 for Manchester United, managed by Matt Busby, and the signing for the Glasgow club Celtic of another Scot, Jock Stein. Within 15 years, under the stewardship of Stein, Celtic would become the first British club to win the European Cup — and a year later, in 1968, Busby's United became the second.

Thus was destiny signposted through 50 years and the baton was passed from generation to generation. How much did those deeds of Stein and Busby inspire the legendary compatriots who followed them – Shankly at Liverpool and Ferguson at Aberdeen and Manchester? Likewise their players: a generation on, the mercurial Belfast wizard George Best handed, to all intents, his club shirt to David Beckham... Just as, you might say, Welshman John Charles passed on his talents to Ryan Giggs...

Again, how much was the dashing grandeur at the wicket of Ian Botham galvanised by Trueman, or the charms of David Gower by May? And the same baton picked up, in his turn, by Nasser Hussain. How much did golfer Tony Jacklin's achievements spur on Nick Faldo and Sandy Lyle... or the daredevil Moss influence those who followed in his slipstream – Hill *pere et fils* Graham and Damon, or the Scots Stewart, Clark and Coulthard? And surely that Celtic fellowship led by Wales's Gareth Edwards and Northern Ireland's Willie John McBride, which so enthused rugby's British Lions in the early 1970s, enkindled the spirits of Neil Jenkins and Martin Johnson in the late Nineties.

Britain won a solitary gold medal at the 1952 Olympics – horseman Harry Llewellyn on Foxhunter. Two years later, young Roger Bannister exhilarated the world when he broke the 4-minute mile barrier — and inspired following generations of British Olympians still acclaimed around the globe... the likes of Chris Brasher, Ann Packer, David Hemery, Mary Peters, Seb Coe, Daley Thompson, Steve Ovett, Linford Christie, Sally Gunnell, Denise Lewis and, Olympia's Olympian, Steve Redgrave, most successful of them all.

Redgrave (now Sir Steve) and Bannister (now Sir Roger) were with the Queen this spring at Buckingham Palace when she lit the relay torch for Manchester's Commonwealth Games: "Sport," she said, "demonstrates the value of co-operation, team work and team spirit... and emphasises how to take victory or defeat with chivalry and good grace."

And though it has changed in the 50 years of her reign, I'd say British sport has achieved precisely that – and she can be as proud of it as it is of her.

Frank Keating is an author and award-winning journalist

Send them victorious: *(clockwise from above) Denise Lewis celebrates her heptathlon Olympic gold in 2000; Steve Redgrave, greatest Olympian of them all; Bobby Moore and team's 1966 World Cup triumph; England captain David Beckham on the ball for the 2002 World Cup; Scots driving forces and World Motor Racing Champions Jim Clark (1963 and 1965) and Jackie Stewart (1969, 1971 and 1973); smiles as Virginia Wade takes the singles title at Wimbledon in Silver Jubilee year; a great stride forward as Roger Bannister breaks the 4-minute mile barrier in 1954.*

Into the new century

As the Queen's Golden Jubilee approached, her biographers took stock: Sarah Bradford said the Queen represents values that people recognise, "courage, decency and a sense of duty… total dedication to her task". Ben Pimlott concluded simply: "She was constant, in a shifting world"

Celebrating her century, *the Queen Mother attended a service of thanksgiving at St Paul's Cathedral (above) in July 2000. She was born on 4 August 1900, and on her 100th birthday 40,000 people gathered to cheer as she came out of Clarence House to receive her birthday card from the Queen. The Queen Mother died on 30 March 2002, just seven weeks after the Queen had lost her sister Princess Margaret.*

Walkabout in the land of walkabout. *In March 2002, while in Australia for the Commonwealth Heads of Government Conference, the Queen met the people of the small town of Kuranda.*

**Fifty years
as Queen** –
*the official Golden
Jubilee portrait by
John Swannell.*

Britain's place in the world

by John Simpson

In 50 years the world has changed out of all recognition. The great colonial empires have disappeared, and the Soviet empire too; technology has effectively wiped out distance; we've become so much more prosperous that even a single parent on income support expects things which half a century ago a millionaire could only have dreamed of. In 1952 dictatorships were in the majority and democracies were rare; not now. Even racism and class distinction, which were dominant everywhere on earth then, are starting to fade.

Still, throughout this whole time, Britain has wrestled with an identity crisis which hasn't yet been resolved. Where do we belong — as a more or less independent power closely attached to America, four times our size, or as a big player within Europe, which still feels foreign to most British people?

Back in 1952 things were very different. We were still basking in the glory of having won the Second World War. We owned more than a fifth of the entire world's territory and governed 20 per cent of its population. Two years earlier, our motor industry had been the world's largest, and our industrial output was second only to America's. We were still the world's foremost technological power, having invented everything from the computer and the jet engine to television. But it was becoming painfully obvious that none of this was going to last. The curve was downwards, and it was getting steeper all the time.

On the Continent, former enemies were starting to unite. Britain had rejected the idea of joining the European Coal and Steel Community, which in 1951 linked a defeated, half-destroyed Germany with several of the countries it had trampled on. The British saw this co-operation as a vague, long-term threat, but felt they were strong enough to stay aloof.

Steadily, the six ECSC countries grew richer. In 1957 they formed themselves into the European Economic Community, popularly known as the Common Market. Britain countered by setting up the European Free Trade Area, but by the early Sixties the EEC was obviously winning. Having failed to beat the Common Market, we tried to join it. President de Gaulle of France saw this as another effort by *les* Anglo-Saxons to disrupt European togetherness, and in 1963 vetoed Britain's membership bid. We were left

Golden wedding celebration *with Prime Minister Tony Blair and Cherie Blair at 10 Downing Street*

drifting for a decade, getting politically and economically weaker by the year. De Gaulle's revenge for his wartime humiliations at the hands of Churchill and Roosevelt was ferocious.

In the wider world, too, it was a humbling time for Britain. In 1956 the British and French staged an ill thought-out attack on Egypt to defend their interests in the Suez Canal, believing they could rely on the US for support. The Americans dealt them a savage blow by siding with Russia and ordering them out of Egypt. The Suez adventure put an end, finally, to Britain's pretensions to be a world power. Within five years most of the British Empire had been given independence: a process which continued until, in 1997, Britain honoured its nineteenth-century treaty with China and handed back Hong Kong. The Empire was finally gone. We were back on our own again.

Nowadays we tend to regard the British Empire as a kind of imperialist smash-and-grab raid. Yet throughout the twentieth century Britain's intention had always been to give its imperial possessions independence, even though this was often dismissed as hypocritical. When the Queen came to the throne Britain had recently become the first country to ratify the European Convention on Human Rights — the first international human rights agreement with any teeth — and made it apply virtually throughout the Empire. (The US, by contrast, had just blocked a similar proposal at the United Nations.) "Personal freedom," wrote a senior British official, "is one of our main contributions to civilization."

Since 1973 when the UK joined the EC our future has mostly, though sometimes with serious misgivings, been seen as lying in Europe. Slowly the psychological wounds of Suez and de Gaulle's veto healed. The British grew used to being a medium-sized power which (in the phrase of a former foreign secretary) punched above its weight. Slowly the economy strengthened, until in 2000 Britain overtook France and became the world's fourth largest economy, after the US, Japan and Germany. London, now a vibrant multi-cultural city, has resumed its old place as the capital of the world.

The British still haven't entirely worked out where we are going; but as the Queen celebrates the fiftieth year of her reign, half a century of gloom and decline seems to be over.

John Simpson is World Affairs Editor of the BBC

Photographs thanks to

Allsport
Alpha
Camera Press
Corbis
Daily Telegraph
David Montgomery
Hulton Getty Picture Collection
Jamaica Observer
LIG Magazine
Mario Testino
Marius Alexander
Michele Jones
Mirrorpix
News International
PA Photos
Popperfoto
Rex Features
Rupert Truman
Tim Graham
Topham Picturepoint

THE QUEEN'S GOLDEN JUBILEE OFFICIAL SOUVENIR PROGRAMME is produced by The Prince's Trust Trading Limited and published by Redwood for the Queen's Golden Jubilee Weekend Trust. **Project team**: Tom Shebbeare, *Chairman* • Deborah Higgins and Justina Marot, *The Prince's Trust* • Caroline Cousins, *The Queen's Golden Jubilee Weekend Trust* • Helen Bayne, *Golden Jubilee Office* • Penny Russell-Smith, *Press Secretary to HM the Queen.*

Editor Gaythorne Silvester **Art director** Stefano Arata **Contributing editor** Philippa Patton **Managing editor** Caroline Birch **Consultant editor** Peter Crookston
Sub Editor Julie Carman **Picture Researchers** Jenny Kraus, Suzanne Hodgart **Researchers** Amie Barker, Charlotte Moggach **Designer** Richard Plastow **Production Controller**
Heather O'Connell **Senior Account Director** Milton Barratt **Account Director** Alex Bagot • **Chief Executive** Michael Potter *Editorial Director* Christopher Ward *Managing Director*
Keith Grainger *Creative Director* Rami Lippa *Director* Sue Thomas

Redwood, 7 St Martin's Place, London WC2N 4HA, UK. Tel: +44 20 7747 0700. Fax: +44 20 7747 0701. Copyright Redwood 2002. All rights reserved. No part of this publication may be reproduced in any material form (including photocopying or storing it in any medium by electronic means) without the written permission of the copyright owner. Applications for the copyright owner's permission to reproduce any part of this publication should be addressed to Redwood at the above address. Opinions expressed are those of the author and not The Prince's Trust Golden Jubilee Committee. Printing St Ives • Colour Reproduction Electronic Solutions • Paper supplied by M-real, Sittingbourne • Distribution COMAG, Highbury House Communications plc. ISBN 0-9517751-2-X

At Buckingham Palace: *the Queen and Prince Philip photographed by Bryan Adams for the Golden Jubilee portfolio.*

The spirit of the future

The Queen's Golden Jubilee is about looking forward as well as back: the following pages celebrate just some of the young people who are already making a difference

Although our selection is limited to eight, there are many, many more young people across the Commonwealth who are helping to shape the future of their country, have risen to a challenge, overcome a difficulty, inspired others, or in some way demonstrated determination and character. One of the strongest examples of such a young person was Nkosi Johnson who died in June 2001 aged 12. He was born with AIDS and was the longest-surviving child with the virus in South Africa. He was a spokesperson for AIDS awareness at a time when there was stigma and fear in the country and was an inspiration through his bravery to others such as Freddie Mubitelela from Zambia who is president of the Young Ambassadors of Positive Living Programme. Many thanks to the British Council and The Prince's Trust in putting us in touch with the young people featured here.

Craig Kielburger children's rights activist CANADA

Craig Kielburger founded the charity Free the Children when he was only 12. Now 19, he continues to fight for children's rights.

Searching for cartoons in his local paper one day, Craig Kielburger's attention was caught by a headline: "Boy, 12, murdered for speaking out against child labor". The child in question had been sold into labour in Pakistan aged four and reading about his fate was a turning point for Craig. "Iqbal Masih and I were the same age, but the differences in our lives shocked me. I knew I had to do something."

Craig gathered a group of friends together to establish Free the Children (FTC) and six months later the 12-year-old found himself addressing 2,000 union members in Toronto, receiving a donation of C$150,000. His 13th birthday was celebrated in Calcutta as he travelled through Asia meeting street children. Since then the charity has amassed 100,000 members in more than 35 countries. Although some adults are involved, all policy decisions are taken by children.

FTC has built 300 schools, two rescue homes, three health clinics and distributed 100,000 school kits and C$2.5m of medical supplies. The charity was recently appointed lead partner to the UN Office of the Special Representative for Children in Armed Conflict.

As well as meeting the late Mother Teresa, the Dalai Lama and Her Majesty The Queen, Craig's supporters include Bishop Desmond Tutu and Oprah Winfrey, on whose TV show he has twice appeared. The activist has even found time to write two books.

"In the future I'd like to be involved in conflict mediation to help avoid wars before they start," says Craig. "I see myself working in human rights at an international level."

Before that, there's the small matter of a university degree to be completed, but no doubt Craig will find a way to squeeze it in.

Courtney Foster charity fundraiser JAMAICA

Since 1992, 15-year-old Courtney Foster, from Kingston, has raised well over J$1,000,000 for needy children and students in Jamaica.

When she read in the paper about the plight of a boy with eye cancer, Courtney Foster vowed to raise funds for his treatment. Taking an exercise book to note down contributions, she appealed to her family and friends for money and even asked her mother for access to funds in her own account. At the time she was just four years old.

So emerged a talent for raising money that Courtney has used to greater and greater effect as she's grown up. In 1994 she founded Kids for Charity and staged a fashion show with friends in aid of a local school with no electricity, raising J$35,000. The next year, the fashion show raised over J$52,000 to pay for the school's water supply, and in 1996, she took up the case of a children's home, Walker's Place of Safety, raising J$110,500 towards reconnecting its water supply. Since then the fashion show has become a

Ruwanthie de Chickera playwright and director SRI LANKA

Ruwanthie de Chickera, 26, from Colombo, is an award-winning playwright and director. She is currently studying on a scholarship for an MA in Applied Theatre at the University of Manchester.

To have your work lauded by the playwright Harold Pinter and the distinguished critic Michael Billington is high praise indeed. All the more so when you are just 21. Such was the honour bestowed on Ruwanthie de Chickera for her play *The Crutch*, which won her the prestigious British Council International New Playwriting Award in 1997 for the best play from South Asia.

Surprisingly, Ruwanthie didn't set out to be a writer from an early age. "At 16, I was literally forced to write a play for an inter-school drama competition," she explains. "It did well, so I had to write one the next year, which was also successful."

She soon developed a passion for the theatre and since then her work has taken her to India, Australia and London, where *The Crutch* was produced at the Royal Court Theatre. As well as writing, Ruwanthie directs plays and runs playwriting workshops for young people with her own theatre company, Stages. Her forthcoming projects include directing a play by new Sri Lankan writers at the Cultural Festival of the Commonwealth Games in Manchester this July.

"My plays are about people's stories and observations, rather than specific themes," says Ruwanthie. As for how she sees her work developing in the future, Ruwanthie is keeping an open mind: "I can only think of what I would not want to be in 10 years' time. I wouldn't want to be complacent, rigid or unquestioning. I wouldn't want to be without ideas or idealism."

lucrative annual fundraiser. "My aim is to help the less fortunate for as long as I am able," Courtney says. "I arrange all the rehearsals and fund-raising events before or after school hours. My reward is seeing the smiles on the faces of the recipients."

Individual pupils, as well as schools, have benefited from Courtney's good works, receiving lunch money and financial help with uniforms and books. In 1997, the death of Courtney's uncle, a doctor, saw her launch the Dr Norman Sinclair Memorial Medical Scholarship, an annual grant of J$150,000 awarded to a medical student at the University of the West Indies. Courtney herself has her sights set on a career as a criminal lawyer and her greatest wish is to meet Bill Clinton.

Accolades have been showered on Courtney for her work, most notably an award from the Jamaican newspaper *The Gleaner*, which awarded her with the Gleaner Honour Award for Voluntary Service.

Natalie du Toit champion swimmer SOUTH AFRICA

Swimmer Natalie du Toit was in training for the 2004 Olympics when her left leg had to be amputated at the knee after a traffic accident. Amazingly, the 17-year-old still has her sights on a medal.

Fate could not have dealt Natalie du Toit's sporting ambitions a much crueller blow when she was riding along a main road, a car pulled out of a parking lot straight into her left leg.

Already a national champion, the Cape Town schoolgirl was in training for Athens 2004. Now, only 15 months after the accident, her ambitions are unchanged, her form is much regained and she is holding her own against other, able-bodied, competitors.

Only nine months after losing her leg, she qualified for the South African senior swimming championships. "I had to shift my focus from the short-distance and individual medley swimming events to long-distance freestyle," Natalie explains. "Training was hard at first because I'd lost so much strength and muscle tone in hospital, but my power in my upper body is building up to compensate for what I've lost in my leg. I've had to adapt my turns and starts, which luckily did not have to change much, other than having to build up strength in my good leg."

Hoping to make the 2004 Olympic squad, the swimmer is also aiming for a medal in Beijing 2008. "I don't really consider myself as disabled," says Natalie, who has been fitted with a prosthetic leg. "After all, I can still walk, run and even ride a bike. Most importantly, of course, I can still swim. I have my faith to thank for that."

Daniel Chima Uchechi football coach NIGERIA

Daniel Chima Uchechi is a 15-year-old schoolboy from Badagri, near Nigeria's border with Benin, and a star volunteer at the Community Action Through Sport (CATS) project.

As World Cup fever sweeps the globe, one young player will be taking a keener interest in his country's performance than most. Daniel Chima Uchechi knows at first-hand the therapeutic powers of football – his work with the CATS project helps disadvantaged young people develop leadership skills and improve community life through sport.

Daniel has to take four buses to reach the project and often stays the night to save the fare home. The eldest of seven, his family is poor and his father has not had a permanent job for two

years. "When I look at my family, I think that by playing football I can help them and others as poor as me," says Daniel. "If things seem difficult, I remember how much depends on me."

Daniel is a coach and mentor to younger CATS footballers. "I tell them an opportunity lost can never be regained. The project has given me confidence and enabled me to go to places and do things I could never have done otherwise."

Although drawn to a career in banking, Daniel would love to be a professional footballer. His inspiration is Nwankwo Kanu, the Nigerian

James Fitzpatrick medical student AUSTRALIA

James Fitzpatrick, 28, is a medical student committed to improving healthcare in Australia's isolated communities. In 2001, he was named Young Australian of the Year.

James Fitzpatrick likes having a lot on his plate. Along with playing the didgeridoo and harmonica, he writes poetry and combines his days on the hospital wards with studying and volunteer work.

"Good people often remind me that family, friends and self-preservation also rank high on the list of life's priorities," he admits.

James's love of the country stems from his days at boarding school in rural New South Wales. This led to agricultural studies in America, but his life changed direction during a stint in the Australian Army, when he pondered "the best way to make a contribution to the world around me". After completing a science degree, he now studies medicine at the University of Western Australia, where he is involved in the SPINRPHEX rural health group, a network of 5,000 students from various medical disciplines.

"Rural patients, especially those in Aboriginal and Torres Strait Islander communities, have higher rates of heart disease, diabetes and infectious diseases," James explains. "Our aim is to create awareness of the need for rural, remote and indigenous healthcare."

Not one to do things by the book, James cites Patch Adams, the unorthodox American doctor who advocated laughter as therapy, as his hero. "He grasped a truth that opposed mainstream healthcare and inspired millions through his strong, practical optimism."

Flexible about his future, James sees himself working in remote Western Australia, with Médecins Sans Frontières abroad, or even in politics. "I have a penchant for freedom," he confesses. "I like going straight when I want to go straight, turning left when I want to go left."

Whatever direction his future takes him, the Young Australian of the Year is determined to "make a difference".

soccer star and Arsenal striker who suffered a life-threatening heart complaint and set up a heart foundation. So which charities would Daniel support himself? "If I won a million dollars I'd give 10 per cent as a tithe because I'm a Christian; $100,000 each to orphans, people with HIV/AIDS and the Ikeja bomb victims; $100,000 to CATS and $100,000 for my family's education. I'd give the rest to my father to invest."

But what about something for himself? "No," says Daniel simply. "If I could do these things, I'd be happy enough."

Growing up among travellers, Vincent Jelinek may not have had a conventional education, but he certainly learnt some useful skills from the 'school of life'. "I've been responsible for my own finances since I was very young," says Vincent. "When I was 12, I set up Vincent's Valeting Service, cleaning people's cars, but there wasn't much of a market for it among travellers and it didn't take off very well!"

A stint with a pyrotechnics circus in Spain proved more successful, when the 14-year-old Vincent made props and fitted out vehicles for the performers. Feeding his growing interest in design, he then enrolled at an Oxfordshire college to take a BTEC National Diploma in Design when he was 15. Vincent excelled on the course and after various woodworking jobs he founded InCreation, a design and furniture business, with support from The Prince's Trust last year. The company's projected turnover was £25,000 but it almost doubled that in its first year.

Vincent's appetite for learning then prompted him to set up a community-based education project in East London, where he lives. "IntaLearning is designed to give young people practical skills and the confidence to apply them in the workplace, as well as encourage them to take part in more education." The informal project focuses on woodwork, making anything from skateboarding ramps to dolls' houses, but

Vincent Jelinek founder of design business UK

The son of New Age travellers, Vincent Jelinek, 22, had no formal education and was brought up in Ireland, France, Spain and around the UK. He now runs a design business and an education project in East London.

Vincent hopes to expand it. "If I had the money, I'd buy a big building with art and music studios, a metal-working space and a games room."

Such drive and vision was recognised at *The Mirror*'s Pride of Britain Awards this year, when Vincent was nominated as the finalist for London in The Prince's Trust Young Achiever category.

Interviews by Helen Saunders

Sorayya Hussain community worker UK

Born in Bradford to Pakistani parents, 26-year-old Sorayya Hussain is a development worker with a masters degree in Urban Regeneration.

Sorayya Hussain leads a double life. By day, she works in urban regeneration for Bradford City Council; in her spare time, she's a tireless volunteer within her local Muslim community. "I've always had two jobs," Sorayya explains. "Whenever I go out, my father asks, 'What is it this time – work, or your voluntary thing?'"

Sorayya first became involved in community work at 16, sitting on her school council. As a student, she joined a discussion group set up after the Manningham riots of 1995. Now she's vice chair of the Bradford Asian Girls Education Association and on a committee for the Asian Women and Girls' Centre in Manningham.

"Our aim is to empower women with

educational and social opportunities. We introduce them to role models who show that becoming an independent, career-minded woman doesn't mean you have to lose your Islamic identity."

Sorayya was most recently involved in the British Council's Connecting Youth project, an international forum for young Muslims. "The forum really broke down stereotypes and challenged preconceptions," says Sorayya. "It was a great opportunity to share global experiences in such a melting pot."

Integration is a key issue for Sorayya, who is inspired by Martin Luther King because, "he campaigned for integration regardless of race and had a vision for future generations".

calendar
of events

THE QUEEN'S
GOLDEN JUBILEE
2002

During the summer of 2002 the Queen and the Duke of Edinburgh are travellir Wales, Northern Ireland and each region of England. The programme is designed to enab includes royal visits to the Commonwealth countries of Jamaica, New Zealand and Australia

The Golden Jubilee presents an occasion for celebration involving the whole community. It provides the Queen with the opportunity to thank the nation and the Commonwealth for their support during her reign. The celebrations are also a time to recognise all those who support and contribute to their communities. The Jubilee offers the chance to reflect on the ways our lives have changed over the past 50 years, to see where we stand today and to look to the future. Celebrating the achievements of young people and the Commonwealth and looking ahead to the contribution of youth to our society are also important aspects of the Jubilee.

29th *The Queen and the Duke of Edinburgh attend dinner at No 10 Downing Street hosted by the Prime Minister.*

30th *The Queen addresses both Houses of Parliament during a session of the Joint Houses of Houses of Parliament in Westminster Hall (subject to approval by each House).*

1st **The South West** *The Queen and the Duke of Edinburgh visit the National Maritime Museum in Falmouth, Cornwall. The Queen views Trelissick gardens, while the Duke of Edinburgh visits Falmouth College of Art. Lunch celebrates the 125th anniversary of the Diocese of Truro. The Queen then meets community representatives in Truro Cathedral. A musical performance in Exeter is followed by a reception hosted by the County of Devon.*

2nd *The Queen and Duke of Edinburgh visit the Farmers' Market and Vivary Park, Taunton then on to Wells where the Duke of Edinburgh presents Award Scheme Gold Awards. Lunch is hosted by Bath and North East Somerset Council at Guildhall. They visit Bath Abbey and attend a reception at the Pump Rooms.*

7th **The North East** *The Queen, accompanied by the Duke of Edinburgh, opens the Winter Gardens in Sunderland and the Metro link between Sunderland and Gateshead. She then visits St Joseph's Roman Catholic Primary School, Fellgate, and officially opens the Millennium Bridge. A visit to the Baltic Centre is followed by a gala event at City Hall, Newcastle.*

8th *The Queen and the Duke of Edinburgh visit Seaham, Easington and Blackhall Rocks. They continue on to Durham Castle; open Millennium Place, Durham; and then visit Darlington. The Duke of Edinburgh will present Award Scheme Gold Awards at Peterlee and visit Stockton Campus, Durham University.*

9th **The South East** *The Queen visits Walthamstow to present Jubilee awards for civic achievement. She travels to Redbridge to see allotments tended by individuals with disabilities. Then follows a reception at West Ham football ground. She then goes to Eastbury Manor House, Barking, while the Duke of Edinburgh visits the University of East London.*

10th *The Queen visits Aylesbury then, with the Duke of Edinburgh, she goes on to Higginson Park, Marlow. She then continues on to Bisham Abbey National Sports Centre.*

april

he length and breadth of the United Kingdom on a Golden Jubilee tour taking in Scotland,
hem to meet as many people as possible throughout the country. The Golden Jubilee year also
ebruary and March and Canada in October.

26th *The Queen, accompanied by the Duke of Edinburgh, attends the General Assembly Service, St Giles' Cathedral, Edinburgh.*

20th *The Queen, accompanied by the Duke of Edinburgh, visits Chelsea Flower Show.*

27th *A trip to some of the more remote parts of Scotland takes in the Isle of Skye* **(pictured);** *lunch at Stornoway, Isle of Lewis; and a tea party at Wick, Caithness.*

21st *The Queen opens the new Queen's Gallery at Buckingham Palace.*

28th *The Royal couple attends Aberdeen's Jubilee Celebration, and the Scottish Parliament, sitting at Aberdeen University. The Queen opens the Scottish School of Contemporary Dance, Dundee, while the Duke of Edinburgh visits Dundee University's Wellcome Trust Biocentre. There is a reception at City Chambers, Dundee.*

22nd *The Royal couple attends an arts reception at the Royal Academy of Arts, London.*

29th *The day includes a visit to Lauder and Melrose Abbey in the Scottish Borders. Lunch, hosted by Scottish Borders Council, is followed by a Borders Gathering at Melrose Rugby Club.*

16th *The Queen and the Duke of Edinburgh attend the Royal Windsor Horse Show.*

23rd **Scotland** *The Queen and the Duke of Edinburgh attend a Thanksgiving Service at Glasgow Cathedral.*

17th *The Queen and the Duke of Edinburgh spend a second day watching events at the Royal Windsor Horse Show.*

24th *The Queen opens the Jubilee Wheel at Millennium Link between Forth & Clyde and Union Canals, Falkirk; she then gives a reception in the Palace of Holyroodhouse for national Scottish figures.*

18th *The Queen takes the salute at 'All The Queen's Horses', Royal Windsor Horse Show.*

25th *The Queen opens the General Assembly of the Church of Scotland, Edinburgh, and gives a garden party at the Palace of Holyroodhouse.*

may

june

The National celebrations over the Jubilee weekend, from the 1st-4th June, are the focal point of the Golden Jubilee. In addition to the State events, The Golden Jubilee Festival in Green Park, St. James Park and The Mall will include national events taking place in London. On Tuesday a series of pageants produced by Sir Michael Parker will take place during the afternoon. The BBC is organising classical and pop concerts in the garden of Buckingham Palace. BBC's Music Live, in addition to its street festivals throughout the country, is staging a centrepiece event in Hyde Park. All events are being televised and big screens along The Mall and in the Buckingham Palace area are broadcasting the events live.

1st Prom at the Palace

The Queen and the Duke of Edinburgh host a classical concert – Prom at the Palace – in the gardens at Buckingham Palace. The BBC Symphony Orchestra and Chorus, under the baton of their Conductor Laureate Sir Andrew Davis will form the backbone of the classical concert. Artists include Russian cellist Mstislav Rostropovich, internationally acclaimed soprano Dame Kiri Te Kanawa and top British baritone Sir Thomas Allen who will sing popular music from opera and musical theatre. Opera's hottest duo, Roberto Alagna and Angela Gheorghiu, make a special appearance performing solos and a duet.

2nd Jubilee Church Service

The Queen and the Duke of Edinburgh attend a Jubilee Church Service, St George's Chapel, Windsor Castle.

3rd The People's Party

At lunchtime bells, drums, whistles and gongs herald the beginning of the Golden Jubilee Summer Party. Fun and festivities will take place across the country with garden and street parties. The Queen and the Duke of Edinburgh spend the morning attending events in Slough and Windsor.

Party at the Palace

The Queen and the Duke of Edinburgh host a pop concert – Party at the Palace – in the gardens at Buckingham Palace. Artists performing represent the past 50 years of popular music and include Eric Clapton, Aretha Franklin, Elton John, Tom Jones, Paul McCartney and Atomic Kitten plus many more. The show is under the creative guidance of Beatles producer Sir George Martin, music producer Phil Ramone and the musical directorship of Michael Kamen.

Lighting the beacon

Escorted by 300 children carrying lanterns, the Queen and the Duke of Edinburgh light the National Beacon in The Mall. The beacon is lit from the Millennium Flame which has been kept alight at St Nicholas Parish Church, Great Yarmouth, since the New Year. Over 650 beacons are part of a network from the Arctic to the Antarctic, Mount Kenya to Nepal, from the Shetlands to Land's End, from Australia to Holyhead and throughout the Commonwealth.

Fireworks and Son et Lumière

The lighting of the beacon sparks a programme of pyrotechnic effects, fireworks and lighting effects including 50 searchlights and 30-foot-high fountains from the Queen Victoria Memorial, accompanied by both classical and modern music. Fireworks are fired from the roof of Buckingham Palace and The Mall as well as Green Park.

jubilee

4th Ceremonial procession

Travelling in the Gold State Coach, the Queen and the Duke of Edinburgh leave Buckingham Palace for a ceremonial procession to St Paul's. Accompanied by over 1,000 musicians playing from two large stages, they will travel down The Mall. The bands include the Orchestra of The Royal College of Music, The Bach Choir, The Morriston Orpheus Choir with the Caldicot Male Voice Choir and part of The Golden Jubilee Gospel Choir plus a specially formed Golden Jubilee Steel Orchestra. They perform "Progress for the Queen", a special arrangement of music and singing from around the UK and the Commonwealth.

Halt at Temple Bar

In keeping with tradition, the Queen halts at Temple Bar where the Lord Mayor of the City of London surrenders the Pearl Sword, a symbol of the City's independence, to the Queen who returns it before proceeding to St Paul's. The route from Temple Bar will be lined by fanfare teams with brass and military bands playing specially arranged music. The Queen and the Duke of Edinburgh then attend a lunch hosted by the Lord Mayor and the Corporation of London at Guildhall in the City of London.

Golden Jubilee National Festival

The Queen and the Duke of Edinburgh watch as processions of fabulously colourful floats and parades progress down The Mall. One of the main events is a cavalcade of moving structures depicting 50 years of British cultural and social history. The 'Service' Parade, of over 2,000, consists of a cross section of organisations and groups who have contributed great service to the country during the Queen's reign. On the theme of 'Yesterday' 'Today' and 'Tomorrow', veterans, heroes and young trainees will join with the current serving members. The Gospel Choir Parade is made up of 5,000 gospel singers from a large number of groups who, having sung their own songs as they move down The Mall, join in the finale around Buckingham Palace. There will be over 2,500 participants in the Notting Hill Carnival Parade from many of the 'Bands' that make up the annual Notting Hill Carnival. The Chicken Shed Children's and Youth Theatre and members of Chicken Shed outreach projects make up 1,000 young people aged 7-18 who represent 'the future' by performing "Together Talking", a song which celebrates the joy and creativity of shared communication.

The final procession

is of 4,000 performers from around Britain and the Commonwealth carrying large rainbow arches made up of 'wishes' and 'hopes' written by children from 74 countries. The children escort the Queen and the Duke of Edinburgh into the Palace forecourt, where the Queen unveils a balcony hanging made by The Royal School of Needlework with the national flags and emblems of all the Commonwealth countries made by children from those countries.

Balcony appearance

The Queen and the Duke of Edinburgh make a balcony appearance at Buckingham Palace and watch an RAF fly-past. A choir of 7,000 with over 1,000 musicians and a crowd, likely to number hundreds of thousands, will join together for massed singing.

june

1st The Queen and the Duke of Edinburgh host Prom at the Palace at Buckingham Palace.

2nd The Queen and the Duke of Edinburgh attend St George's Chapel, Windsor Castle.

3rd The Queen and the Duke of Edinburgh attend events in Windsor and Slough. The Royal couple host Party at the Palace at Buckingham Palace, and light a National Beacon in The Mall.

4th The Royal couple attends a National Service of Thanksgiving at St Paul's, after a ceremonial procession from Buckingham Palace. The Lord Mayor and the Corporation of London host a lunch at Guildhall in the City. This is followed by the Golden Jubilee Festival in The Mall and includes a balcony appearance to watch an RAF fly-past. (For full details of the Golden Jubilee Weekend see previous page.)

6th The Queen visits a bus depot in Brent to thank employees for working through the Golden Jubilee Central Weekend. The Royal couple goes on to Barnet to view a parade representing north London communities. This is followed by a reception at the Alexandra Palace in Haringey, and a garden party at Lambeth Palace.

7th The Queen, accompanied by the Duke of Edinburgh, attends the South of England Show at Ardingly in West Sussex.

15th *The Queen takes the salute at Her Majesty's Birthday Parade, Horseguards.*

10th *The Queen and the Duke of Edinburgh give a reception for representatives of different faiths at Buckingham Palace.*

17th *The Queen and the Duke of Edinburgh attend the service of the Order of the Garter at St George's Chapel, Windsor. Later they give a dinner for European Sovereigns at Windsor.*

11th **Wales** *After arriving at Llanfairpwll railway station, the Queen and the Duke of Edinburgh visit a crafts exhibition and fair at Beaumaris Castle, Anglesey. Afterwards they attend a Thanksgiving Service at Bangor Cathedral, attend lunch hosted by the National Trust Wales and the Chairman of Gwynedd County Council at Penrhyn Castle, followed by a Jubilee sports event in Colwyn Bay.*

18th *The Queen and the Duke of Edinburgh attend Royal Ascot* **(pictured)** *until 22 June.*

25th *The Royal couple visits Uxbridge where the Queen unveils the statue 'Anticipation' by Anita Lafford. They then visit Gunnersbury Park to meet representatives of west London boroughs before going to All Saints Parish Church, Kingston-upon-Thames, where the Queen unveils a stone commemorating the 1100th anniversary of the coronation in Kingston of King Edward the Elder. They then travel to Bushy Park.*

12th *The Royal couple attends the Powys picnic, Dolau; open improvement works, a new lock at Burry Port Harbour and the Millennium Coastal Park, Llanelli. Carmarthenshire County Council host a lunch. A visit to Carmarthenshire Enterprise Day is followed by the Festival of Youth and Community Service at Margram Park.*

26th *The Queen and the Duke of Edinburgh host a dinner for representatives of the Armed Services at Windsor Castle.*

13th *The Royal couple drives through Bridgend shopping centre; attends Welcome to the Valleys at Treorchi, Rhondda Valley; visits Heritage Park, Trehafod, Porth; attends a lunch with Newport County Borough Council; visits the National Assembly of Wales; and attends a reception hosted by Cardiff City Council.*

27th *The Royal couple visits the Armed Forces in Portsmouth during their visit to the south coast city.*

2nd **West Midlands** *The visit includes Touchwood, Solihull's town centre redevelopment. The Queen opens Millennium Point Science and Learning Centre, Digbeth, Birmingham. In the evening there is a reception and concert in Symphony Hall, Birmingham.*

9th **The South East** *Buckingham Palace plays host to the winners of The Queen's Golden Jubilee Poetry Competition for Schools. This is followed by a garden party in the gardens of Buckingham Palace, where guests include those born on Accession Day.*

16th *The Queen and the Duke of Edinburgh host a garden party at Buckingham Palace. Guests include young people born since the 1977 Silver Jubilee.*

3rd *The Royal couple visits the National Museum of Brewing, Burton upon Trent, after which the Queen visits Brewhouse Arts Centre, while the Duke of Edinburgh visits Best Foods' Marmite factory. They both visit the National Memorial Arboretum, Alrewas, Staffordshire, and the Royal Show, Stoneleigh, Warwickshire.*

11th **Yorkshire** *The Queen visits Leeds Civic Centre and the set of TV soap "Emmerdale". The Royal couple joins Jubilee celebrations at Harewood House. The Queen meets the Golden Jubilee Baton relay runners. The Duke of Edinburgh visits the National Coal Mining Museum and Bradford Grammar School.*

17th **East Anglia** *Suffolk plays host to the Queen and the Duke of Edinburgh when they visit Ipswich and Stowmarket; this is followed by a lunch in Bury St Edmunds and a performance in Abbey Gardens, Bury St Edmunds.*

4th *The Queen and the Duke of Edinburgh visit the refurbished Broadway Theatre in Lewisham before travelling to Croydon's BRIT School for Performing Arts and Technology, this is followed by a reception at Addington Palace. The Queen goes on to the sports centre at Crystal Palace Park to watch the London Youth 'Mini' Games.*

12th *A service for rural life at Beverley Minster is followed by a visit by the Royal couple to Beverley Racecourse for a County Fair and Golden Jubilee Race.*

18th *The Queen and the Duke of Edinburgh visit Norwich Castle Museum after which the Queen opens the Forum Building (the Norfolk and Norwich Millennium Library), Norwich. The Duke of Edinburgh opens the Norfolk Nelson Museum, Great Yarmouth. They then give a garden party at Sandringham House.*

5th *The Queen and the Duke of Edinburgh attend a parade in the gardens of Buckingham Palace for all Her Majesty's bodyguards and the in-pensioners of the Royal Hospital Chelsea.*

july

23rd The South East *The Queen, accompanied by the Duke of Edinburgh, opens the new Greater London Authority Building followed by a gala at Covent Garden.*

24th The North West *The Queen visits King's School, Macclesfield and the Christie Hospital, Greater Manchester. The Queen and the Duke of Edinburgh attend a service celebrating the new city centre at Manchester Cathedral. The Duke of Edinburgh opens the Imperial War Museum North.*

25th *The Queen visits the Walker Art Gallery, Liverpool, while the Duke of Edinburgh presents Award Scheme Gold Awards at the Town Hall, Bootle, Liverpool. They attend a reception at the Walker Art Gallery and visit Liverpool Town Hall. The Queen then opens the Commonwealth Games, Greater Manchester.*

26th *The Queen and the Duke of Edinburgh visit the Commonwealth Games sports venues and Athletes' Village, Greater Manchester.*

30th *A garden party in the gardens of Buckingham Palace includes representatives of charities of which the Queen and the Duke of Edinburgh are patrons.*

31st East Midlands *The Queen opens Lindsey Lodge Hospice Extension, Scunthorpe; the Royal couple visits Scunthorpe Town Centre, Normanby Hall and attends the National Ice Centre, Nottingham. The Duke of Edinburgh presents Award Scheme Gold Awards at 20/21 Arts Centre, Scunthorpe.*

1st *The Queen and the Duke of Edinburgh visit Leicester city centre. This is followed by a visit to the National Space Centre, Leicester; and a celebration at Pride Park, Derby.*

4th The North West *The Queen closes the Commonwealth Games, Manchester.*

5th *The Royal couple attends a community event, and a reception in Preston followed by a garden party at Carlisle Castle in Cumbria. Continuing north they attend the Edinburgh Military Tattoo, Edinburgh Castle (**pictured**).*

7th *The Queen and the Duke of Edinburgh host a garden party at Balmoral Castle.*

august

The organisers of the Queen's Golden Jubilee weekend would

like to thank the following companies, trusts and individuals

who generously supported the Jubilee celebrations and events

Abbey National Group
Allied Irish Bank (GB)
Alpha Airports Group Plc
Alpha Bank
AMEC plc
Anglo American plc
Anglo Irish Bank Corporation Plc
ANZ Investment Bank
BAE SYSTEMS plc
The Baltic Exchange
Bank Leumi (UK) plc
Bank of Baroda
The Bank of East Asia, Limited
Bank of India
Bank of Montreal
Sir David and Sir Fredrick Barclay
Barclays PLC
Bayerische Hypo- und Vereinsbank AG
J L Beckwith Charitable Trust
BNP Paribas
BP plc
BP Shipping
Bradford & Bingley plc
Bristol & West plc
British Airways Plc
The British Land Company plc
Buckingham Foods
C Hoare & Co
Cadogan Estates Limited
Caledonia Investments plc
Canara Bank
Canary Wharf Group plc
Capespan Limited
Dr Massimo Carello
Centrica plc
The Chamber of Shipping
Chime Communications PLC
Citigroup
Close Brothers Limited
Commonwealth Bank of Australia
Compass Group PLC
Consignia

The Co-operative Bank plc
Corus Group plc
Credit Lyonnais
Credit Suisse First Boston (Europe) Limited
Den norske Bank ASA London Branch
Deutsche Bank AG
Dixons Group plc
Sir Harry Djanogly CBE
Egg
Enterprise Oil plc
F&C Smaller Companies PLC
Ford Motor Company Ltd
Fortis Bank
Freshfields Bruckhaus Deringer
Garfield Weston Foundation
Gerald Eve
GKN plc
Gosling Foundation
Grosvenor
GUS Charitable Trust
Halifax and Bank of Scotland
Hamburgische Landesbank
Haymarket Publishing Group
Sir Jack Hayward
Healey & Baker
HFC Bank plc
Highbury House Communications PLC
HSBC Bank plc
HSS Hire Service Group PLC
ICI
Investec Bank (UK) Limited
J P Morgan
JC Bamford Excavators Ltd
Kellogg's
King Sturge
Kingfisher plc
KPMG
KPMG Consulting
Land Securities PLC
Lazard
Linbury Trust
Lloyd's of London

Lloyds TSB Group plc
Man Group plc
Mayday Group
Mitsubishi Group Companies - UK
Moscow Narodny Bank Limited
National Australia Group
National Bank of Abu Dhabi
The National Lottery
Nationwide Building Society
Nestle Food Services
Newbury Building Society
OyezStraker Office Supplies
P&O Cruises
P&O Nedlloyd
P&O Stena Line
Philips Electronics UK Ltd
Mr Bruno Peek OBE
Peninsular & Oriental Steam Navigation
Company
Prudential plc
RAC Motoring Services
Rentokil Initial Plc
Royal & Sun Alliance Insurance plc
The Royal Bank of Scotland Group
Sainsbury's Bank
Shell UK
Six Continents plc
South African Breweries plc
Standard Chartered plc
Stena
Superior Foods Ltd
Swedbank
John Swire & Sons Ltd
United Biscuits Ltd
United Mizrahi Bank Limited
Vodafone Group plc
Walkers Snackfoods Ltd
The Weinburg Foundation
Wightlink Limited
WPP Group plc
WS Atkins plc
Yahoo!